Endors

As someone who was highly challenged with Math in school and declared herself as "not good at math", this book is THE answer to our students no longer saying that! The nuggets of genius that Jonily has included in this book should be in every classroom. Every. Single. One.

—LaVonna Roth, Chief Illuminator,
Author & Speaker for Ignite Your S.H.I.N.E®

Jonily is all about Making Mathineers. Her stories are relatable, and her passion is infectious. She shows us that every student has their own mathematical story within them. This groundbreaking book will change the way we know and do math.

—Kary Oberbrunner Author of Elixir Project and
Day Job to Dream Job

MAKING MATHINEERS

TRANSFORMATIONAL MATH EXPERIENCES THAT BUILD CONCEPTUAL THINKING FOR BOTH THE TEACHER AND THE STUDENT.

Make it Happen!

JONILY ZUPANCIC
WITH APRIL TRIBE GIAUQUE

AUTHOR ACADEMY elite

Making Mathineers
Copyright © 2020 by Jonily Zupancic with April Tribe Giauque.

No part of this publication may be reproduced, stored in a retrieval system, or transmitted in any form or by any means—for example, electronic, photo-copy, recording—without the prior written permission of the publisher, Author Academy Elite. Mindsonmath.com

Paperback: 978-1-64746-492-9
Hardback: 978-1-64746-493-6
Ebook: 978-1-64746-494-3
Library of Congress Control Number: 2020917112

FOREWORD

Welcome fellow educators! My name is Pat Quinn and for the past two decades I have been helping create school environments where all students can be successful. As a classroom teacher with years of experience at the elementary, middle, and high school levels, I have seen many programs come and go through my district, my school, and my classroom. Like many of you, I often shake my head when the names of the programs change, but the results do not. Year in and year out there are students who struggle to learn, survive, and succeed.

As the author of two bestselling books about creating classrooms where all students can thrive, I spend time traveling the country helping teachers and schools design better learning environments. About ten years ago I started to hear one name mentioned at multiple schools in which I worked. Her name was attached to words like *common sense, teacher-friendly*, and *realistic*. When I asked who they were talking about, the answer was always, Jonily!

I knew if there was this much grassroots support from teachers for someone who was sharing their craft, this must be good. So I made the trip to Ohio to check Jonily out. I was *not* disappointed.

Jonily Zupancic is a force to be reckoned with. She is truly a classroom teacher. She has the ability to communicate how teaching techniques she is using can easily be replicated by any educator. I have personally witnessed first-year teachers and 30-year veterans both using Jonily's strategies in the same school! Across different curriculum, standards, states, and systems, her methods have been tried and tested and have proven to work for all students!

The world of improving math instruction is filled with researchers who study techniques in sterile settings that do not survive the transition to the chaos of a real classroom. These well-meaning academics have the luxury of controlling the variables that a classroom teacher simply does not.

Schools around the country are also dotted with superstar math teachers who have some sort of "magic" that makes their students succeed while other students do not. Unfortunately, either this cult-like personality is impossible to duplicate by other teachers, or the superstars themselves are unable to communicate what they are doing in a way that is meaningful to other teachers.

Jonily is the exception to both rules. Certainly, she is a superstar teacher, but not due to any "magic" not accessible to other teachers, (unless you count her smile)! Her techniques are proven to work in actual classrooms with lively students and real chaos that happens every day.

Because of this, Jonily Zupancic is uniquely qualified to write this book, Making Mathineers. This book is one of the few I would recommend to any teacher serious about reaching all students.

Math is a gateway to high-paying jobs and a future filled with opportunities and options. To deny this opportunity to a portion of our students because of a lack of time, resources or willingness to change is not acceptable. In a world where the advice coming from experts is often unrealistic or untested, Jonily fills these pages with simple strategies and techniques that open up the world of math to all students in all our classrooms. Jonily's focus to make every student a Mathineer is the power of this book.

I cannot wait to get started!

—Pat Quinn
Author and Speaker at PatQuinn.com

DEDICATION

To my mom, dad, and Ryan for your unconditional support and for always cheering me on. To my kids, Anden and Baylor. You have been the driving force of making me the Mathineer I am today. Not only do I see math differently because of you, I see the world differently because of your perspective. You are the inspiration for my work. And finally, to the teachers and students I have had the opportunity to learn from over the past 20 years. Thank you for the wealth of mathematical knowledge I now have!

TABLE OF CONTENTS

Strategies: It's a Chicken and Egg Thing. 105

**Success: Watching the Plots
on the Quadrant Move! 175**

INTRODUCTION

Language is human communication through any of three methods that consist of the use of words in a structured way. These methods include spoken, written, and signed communication used by communities and countries. Without language, we would struggle to convey our needs and desires. In fact, we would lack the ability to learn from each other and teach our next generation.

Our stories are told through language, each person's life is a story, compiled through experience and perspective. When you return home from a day of teaching, a family member may ask, "How was your day?" You might respond by sharing a story about a student, an incident on the playground, or something crazy that happened in math class. We are programmed to learn through stories.

Math loves stories. Our lives are replete with story and word problems, and if you are thinking that this book is full of all the tips and tricks on how to solve them, you're wrong. We don't need tips and tricks, vocabulary memorization strategies, or step by step linear approaches. There's a new story to tell, designed to bring you a mathematical experience you won't be able to forget.

Through the use of stories, you will experience Number Sense and what it truly is versus what you may perceive as Math Ability. Buckle up as we go through stories of the ups and downs of students and their teachers. I can't wait for you to improve your own and your students' Number Sense and Math Abilities! Experience the *stories* of students and teachers, discover *symptoms*, teach *strategies and* find *success* for all students! Are you Ready? Here we go!

STORIES

THROUGH LANGUAGE, STORIES DRAW US IN. MATH STORIES ARE NO DIFFERENT.

1
QUADRANT & LANGUAGE: A QUICK HISTORY

LANGUAGE. WHAT IS it? It is human communication through speaking, writing, or signing that consists of the use of words in a structured way. It is a system of communication used by a community or a country. Without language, we can't get our wants and needs met. We can't share our desires with others, and we will struggle to learn anything. Language, in whatever form, allows us to express our wants and needs, and includes the discourse of math.

Many cultures provide people with an understanding of numbers through their language. They teach a word that represents each number, like one, two, three, four, five, and so forth to ten. Words that continue beyond ten are also represented in every language. There are structures and sets of rules in many languages that use the ten-rule, and also some that don't.

In English, what comes after ten? Eleven, twelve, thirteen, fourteen, and so forth. However, there are many languages in the world that teach counting beyond ten using a consistent pattern of combining tens and ones, such as in Chinese and Russian. In these languages, eleven and twelve follow a pattern that helps learners visualize what occurs after 10—ten plus one. It's different and easier to grasp than what occurs in English. Eleven and twelve are words that don't follow a number structure.

In Chinese and Russian, the number for the English word eleven is a structure that includes the number ten: Ten plus 1, ten plus 2, ten plus 3; only in this context we get to leave out the word "plus." The counting then becomes 1 ten 1, 1 ten 2 and so forth, until twenty, which is two tens plus zero, or 2 ten 0, and twenty-one, which is 2 ten 1. In German, as in English, the first two numbers following ten also don't fit the pattern but everything from thirteen and up do. The numbers structured beyond the tens remain in that structure through hundreds, thousands, and so forth. It's easier to think about what is being represented in this structure.

In Chinese, Russian, and German, children learn as tiny toddlers that there is place value and structure to numbers. Thankfully, it's more than just memorizing or rote counting. They are learning to add one from the base to a set of ten each time you count up, and the language supports the structure because they repeat the word "ten" with each count. The language gives mathematics a sense of connection to the operation of number and value right from the start.

I had been teaching for a few years before my son, Anden, was born. I had a strong sense of numbering by this time. I wanted to make sure my son had this as well. When he was a toddler, I taught him how to count using the same structure as the Chinese do: 1 ten 1, 1 ten 2, etc. instead of eleven and twelve We did it every time we counted anything. The same rule applies for twenties: 2 ten 1, 2 ten 2; thirties: 3 ten 1, 3 ten 2 and so forth.

He took off with it and counted in this manner when we were in the car, at home, or out in the community. We did it forward and backward up and down until it became his permanent Number Sense. We played with ten's and stacks of one hundreds. We played games with a 120 chart as well. It wasn't until Anden started preschool that he learned the words eleven and twelve. But because he had a strong sense of number and counting with language that gave him an innate understanding of number connection to operation and place value, he started school way ahead of the game.

When Anden was in first grade, I asked him how many numbers there were in multiple hundred charts. He answered, 500, 600, 700, 800, 900 because since he understood the language, he could replace it with the correct word. When he got to the word 1,000, he said, "10 hundred, 11 hundred, 12 hundred, 13 hundred," then continued with, "20 hundred, 30 hundred," and so forth. Imagine your first graders understanding the same structure. This wasn't done by memorization, but by practicing counting during many small interactions over time wherein the pattern and place value already built in was repeated over and over. Language is key to understanding mathematics!

Think about the structure of numbers in the English language, and how counting things at home, around town, while driving, and counting forward and backward can give a tight structure for kiddos to ground their Number Sense prior to starting school.

This structure creates a different perspective and accessibility for many young students.

For example:
To add the numbers 38+47 (using language)
We would say: 3 ten 8 and 4 ten 7

Add 3 ten and 4 ten, which is 7 ten.
Add 7 and 8 which is 1 ten 5.
Now we have 7 ten 1 ten 5,
which is 8 ten 5,
which is 85.

Different thinking and processing than the traditional algorithm most of us are familiar with can make counting (and operation) a breeze.

● ● ●

The Quadrant

As many of you know, the coordinate plane was developed centuries ago by the French mathematician, René Descartes. In his honor, the system is sometimes called the "Cartesian Coordinate System." In mathematics, we use the coordinate plane to plot points and graph lines. This system allows us to describe algebraic relationships in a visual sense, and also helps us create and interpret algebraic concepts.

Deep breath everyone. I think I can hear my K-5 teachers say something like this, "Okay, wait. Hold up. We were just talking about different languages and base and ease of counting. Now we're suddenly in algebra?" Yes! Let me share why. Algebra, function, and rate are methods of efficient counting and that was what we were doing. But we will discuss more about that later. For now, let's stick to understanding coordinate planes and quadrants for the purpose of this book.

Intersecting x-and y-axes divides the coordinate plane into four sections, or quadrants. The quadrants are named using the Roman numerals I, II, III, and IV beginning with the top right section and moving around in a counterclockwise fashion. This gives us a horizontal line, or axis, called the x-axis, and a vertical axis called the y-axis. The two intersect at the origin or (0, 0). For this book, we are going to rename the x-axis "Number Sense" and the y-axis "Math Ability."

The locations on coordinate planes are described as ordered pairs of numbers telling us the location of a point by relating the point's location along the x-axis (or Number Sense) and along the y-axis (Math Ability). See figure 1.1

Figure 1.1

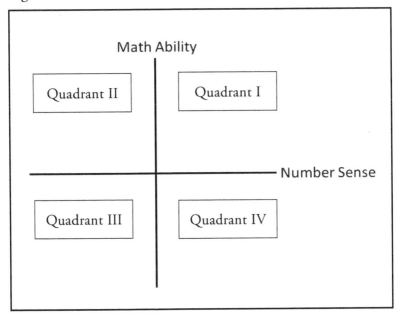

Before we move on, I'd like to define Math Ability and Number Sense. This history and research are vital to setting the stage for everything I teach, so pay attention!

Math Ability is something that is taught and influenced through language, culture, and school learning. I also call it *school math.* Do students know procedures and their facts? Procedures and facts are things like adding and subtracting stacks of numbers and using algorithms. These methods are honored in the school system, and if students struggle with knowing these facts, like multiplication tables, they may start to believe they can't do math.

Number Sense is universal—an innate sense of numbers. Number Sense is conceptual understanding. We all are born with varying degrees of skill acquisition sense, just as people have differing abilities at art, athletics, or science. Number Sense is a group of skills we are innately born with, allowing us to work with numbers and make sense of numbers. It includes skills like:

- Understanding quantities and values, like more or less and larger or smaller (magnitude).
- Recognizing relationships between single items and groups of items (*five* means one group of five items).
- Understanding symbols that represent quantities (*5* means the same thing as *five*).
- Making number comparisons (13 is greater than 10, and three is half of six).
- Understanding the order of numbers in a list: 1st, 2nd, 3rd, etc.

Number Sense is something that can be improved but it isn't done through procedures and fact memorization; it is done through experiences.

Math Ability and Number Sense come from research done at Johns Hopkins by the psychologist, Melissa Libertus. She and her team wanted to find out if children are born with an innate ability for math. They studied 200 four-year-old children (on average) performing tasks that measured Number Sense, mathematical ability, and verbal ability. (Halberda 2011).

In one task, researchers flashed a series of dots on a screen and the children were asked to choose the group of colored dots that were more numerous. The children weren't able to count because the dots were flashed too quickly. The preschoolers would then tell the tester verbally if the blue dots or the yellow dots were more numerous.

The children were also given a standardized test of early mathematics ability that measures the following skills: number comparison, number literacy, mastery of number facts, calculation skills, and number concepts.

Finally, the parents or guardians of the children were given an assessment asking them to indicate whether or not their children used (verbally) any of the math words on the list.

Language and math abilities can be linked through general intelligence, and Libertus wanted to make sure the apparent differences in children's Math Ability did not just evaluate test performance but showed whether the children actually used these terms.

What was the conclusion? Math Ability in preschool children is strongly linked to their inborn primitive Number Sense called Approximate Number System (ANS). "The relationship between Number Sense and Math Ability is important and intriguing because we believe that Number Sense is universal, whereas Math Ability has been thought to be highly dependent on culture and language and takes many years to learn."—Melissa Libertus (Lisa DeNike 2011) (Halberda 2011).

So, hang on. Do we all have a born sense of numbers within us? Yes! Can we improve it with math experiences? Yes! That is what this whole book is about—for you to gain the "Mathematical Experience!" I think I have your attention. Let's have you focus on figure 1.2, which shows the coordinate plane and quadrants.

Figure 1.2

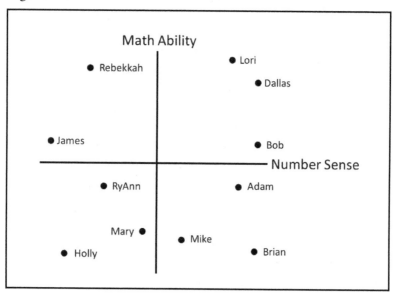

You can see that Number Sense (conceptual math) and Math Ability (procedural math) have replaced the x-and y-axis. Look at how students are placed within the Quadrants. Get familiar with these names and where they are plotted in the Quadrants. We are going to follow these 11 fascinating students as we experience numbers with them. Their stories will reveal the symptoms they have, why they are plotted in their Quadrant, the strategies and mathematical experiences they need to help them improve, and the successful outcome they (and all the students you teach) can obtain. Here we go!

2
STUDENTS—MATH ABILITY AND NUMBER SENSE

STUDENTS' MATH ABILITY and Number Sense speak volumes. Meet the students who will represent the students you find in your everyday classrooms: from public to private schools, from urban to rural, and everything in between. We have a student for you.

What is a school without students? It's nothing. Students are the reason for everything we as teachers do. As math teachers, I'm sure you have many students who seem to fit into each of the Quadrants from our coordinate plane of Math Ability and Number Sense.

Take a look at the figure again and get familiar with the students' placements. In chapters five through eight, we are going to take a deep dive into the Quadrants and why I feel the students are placed where they are.

For the purposes of this book, we are going to focus on these eleven students and their math experience, but only 10 in this chapter, or 1 ten 1, students (just checking to see if you read chapter 1 first). We will meet Rebekkah a little later in Chapter 4. They are going to introduce themselves to you and share what they like to do so you can get to know them and watch their math experience unfold.

QI (Chapter 5)	QII (Chapter 8)	QIII (Chapter 7)	QIV (Chapter 6)
Bob Dallas Lori	Rebekkah James	Holly Mary RyAnn	Adam Brian Mike

This is a snapshot of each student who will be going on their transformational journey of becoming a Mathineer. Some we will meet in elementary school and some at the secondary level. The point about meeting them in different settings is to show the progress and journey we are all on. Introductions will be alphabetically by their first name to help you keep track of them.

● ● ●

Adam

I would describe Adam as a short kid who is a little round, kind of pudgy, and wears glasses. He has a great smile and just fills you up when you see him—he has a zest and zeal for life!

"What's your name?"

"Um, hi. I'm Adam."

"What grade are you in?"

"Second grade."

"Tell me something you like about school."

"I dunno. I guess I like recess. But I sometimes like math. But I mostly like recess. I don't really like wearing my glasses. They really bug me when I go to recess because I like to slide on the slide, and when I slide I like to crash into my friends and my glasses always get knocked off."

"Oh, that's a bummer."

"My mom gets mad because I usually am breaking my glasses, or they get bumped off and then break and stuff. Then she's mad because glasses cost money and she says I need to get a job to pay for my glasses. It's not my fault, really, because I need to be careful and stuff. But recess is the best at school 'cause crashing into my friends is super fun!"

"That is great. Thanks for helping me to answer a few questions."

"Ok. Yeah. Can I go get a drink?"

"Sure. Thanks!"

Adam walks off and gets his drink. As I teach class, he gives me some long looks. I think we are starting a mathematical relationship.

● ● ●

Bob

Since B is the next letter in the alphabet, let's meet Bob, then Brian. Bob has brown hair. He is a little on the skinny side and also wears glasses.

"Hi Bob. I'm wondering if you can help me out?"

"Sure."

"I'd like to ask you a few quick questions."

"Okay."

"What grade are you in?"

"Second grade."

"Cool! What do you like about second grade?"

"I think I like the bigger classroom because we have a reading nook that is so cool. When I get my work done, I go into the nook and get to read, so it's like a little freedom."

"Freedom. Well that is pretty awesome. So, what else do you like about second grade?"

"I kinda like math."

"What do you mean 'kinda like math?'"

"Oh, well, I think it's because numbers just make sense."

"What do you mean that numbers 'just make sense?'"

"Well, when I count, I see numbers going to the right, from zero, and then numbers going to the left."

"What do you mean that you can see numbers?"

"Well, it's like a picture and they stretch out so I can count on to the right forever and then if I look behind me, I see them stretch to the left behind me. I know there are numbers between numbers and numbers. It's just cool. I just know what will come next. I guess because I can see it."

"That is pretty neat. Do you know that that is unique?"

"I guess so."

"Thanks for answering a few of my questions."

And Bob walks off, headed toward the reading nook. I realize he's done talking about math.

● ● ●

Brian

For this fellow, the setting is in middle school. I met Brian during sixth grade, and he has made some incredible changes since then.

Just to give a little background, Brian is a student that has emotional challenges: his parents are divorced, he attends a title I school, and comes from a low socio-economic background as well. He has needed social supports and behavior plans to help him handle the structure and routine of school. Let's just say his home life is challenging and not as consistent as one would like. Sometimes when a student has been identified as having high behavioral needs, generally those needs are the first focus, and then the academic learning. Is the academic gap caused by a learning challenge or by the behavior itself? It depends on the student. For Brian, his behavior has impeded his academic learning.

When I worked with Brian, starting in 6th grade, I wanted to find out his Math Ability and his Number Sense, so I went in big and I went in deep. I discovered that he was in a completely different Quadrant than the one in which his teachers had placed him.

"Hey Brian, how are you?"

"Fine."

"It's great to see you. It's been a little while. Do you mind if I ask you a few questions?"

"Um, ok."

"How's eighth grade going?"

"Well, fine and stuff. Better than 6th grade. I guess 7th grade wasn't too bad. But 8th grade is a little better, I guess."

"Good, glad to hear it. Can I ask you a few math-focused questions?"

"Um, ok."

"How do you work with numbers best? In your head or with paper?"

"In my head."

"Why is that?"

"I guess I can see chunks of things and stuff. And it's like my way of thinking, so I totally get it. When I talk to you, I can tell you the numbers and stuff and you get it. Like in

5th grade, the teachers didn't help and stuff because I had to write things down and stack numbers. I hated crap like that."

"Why did you hate it?"

"Because I wished they could just see how I get it in my head. I mean, something that you've helped me with has started to work a lot better. I just wish I could do more of that stuff."

"How is your math going now?"

"Well, it's better. I'm not as frustrated and stuff. I get my work done. I can stay up with the class too, so that's cool."

"That is cool. Thanks for talking with me."

"Yeah. Sure."

● ● ●

Dallas

Let's stay in middle school, and I'd like to introduce you to Dallas.

"Hey, Dallas, how are you doing?"

"I'm fantastic. How are you?"

"I'm great. Thanks for asking. So, I wanted to find out a few things about you. What is something that I would never know about you?"

"Oh, I like this question. You'll never guess what it is. I'll give you three tries, with only one clue."

"Ok! I'm ready. What is the clue?"

"Pee Wee".

"Pee Wee?" *I giggle out loud! I can't help it.*

"Ok. Let me think. Pee Wee means small, so it has to do with something small and possibly with sports—like a Pee Wee league. Am I close?"

"Hmm, yes. That's a great place to start. You're right to some extent."

"Since you gave me a hint, can I ask a question?"

"Yes."

"For the sport aspect, would it be something that is played with a small hard ball?"

"Yes!"

"I'm going to guess something to do with mini golf!" *His face fell a bit and then rose as if to share something he thought I was never going to guess.*

"Am I right?"

"Yes. It has to do with mini golf, but I have to tell you the best part. My dad and I built a mini golf course in our backyard."

This time my eyes widened. I wanted to know more!

"Really? This is so cool! I have never heard of anyone building one in their backyard. That is impressive!"

"Thanks. It was so much fun designing the course. I loved making pitch and roll of the green, the obstacles players have to putt through, and painting the props. Best way to spend my summer."

"I'd love to see a picture of it."

"Ok. yes. I'll show you a picture."

"Thanks so much. I've learned something incredible today."

"You're welcome."

● ● ●

Holly

Next, we go back to the elementary school setting where we find Holly. She is average sized for her age, and she has long blond hair.

"Morning Holly. How are you?" *A small whisper escapes her.*

"Fine."

"That is good to hear." *She gives me a small glance and I can see her shoulders start to round forward as if to shut me out already.*

"I'm wondering if you wouldn't mind if I just chat with you for a few minutes. Tell me what you like best about school?" *She tosses her long blond ponytail behind her left shoulder and gives me a look like, "Really?" I look right back at her and move the papers aside. Something seems to shift inside her, and she seems to take on a whole new persona. This time, in a stronger voice, she responds.*

"I love lunchtime. I can tell all my friends all the best stuff about whatever I want, and I don't have to do any work. I love my friends at school.

"We like to play games and talk about tons of stuff. Like the other day we were talking about the cutest boys in the school and why they were cute and everything. It was like the best lunch ever."

I knew she had more to say than she ever reveals during math. There is spunk to her after all. But, wow! When math starts, I've never seen a more passive student.

● ● ●

James

Our next student is a girl named James. She is in an interesting academic situation because she attends a private school where Individualized Education Plans (IEP) are not required. However, she had a few challenges, and the team felt they should create an education math plan for her.

"Hello, my Mathineer! How are you doing?"

"I'm ok. Today is a little crazy, but I think I'm good." *With an invitation like that, I will have to ask more about her life.*

"What makes things crazy today?"

"I have to finish my ELA project with my team. I hope I did my part right. I did everything I could think to do, but you know, sometimes I just never know how it will really be accepted and stuff. And then I have a volleyball game after school that I'm kind of freaking out about, because last game I completely messed up. And then I have to get my homework done. I mean yuck . . . it's just a lot." *I could see she wanted to say more, but she stopped herself. So, I pressed on with a few questions.*

"I noticed in math the other day, that you were fast on your facts and got right down to work. That is fantastic, but what happens when you start to feel you might not know the answer?" *She started to shift a little in her seat. Not knowing the answer for someone like James is tough to accept. I mean, she should simply get the answer and then move on. No real thinking or worries, right?*

"Well, I . . . I feel a little like butterflies in my stomach if I can't find the right answer. I really want to just get it done, and not knowing feels really like, yuck. Ya know what I mean?"

"I do. Thanks for sharing that with me."

● ● ●

Lori

Lori is also in middle school. Her skinny, long legs barely fit under the desk, and the length of her dark hair falls to the middle of the chair she sits on.

I notice that as she writes, her glasses seem to slide down the bridge of her nose just a little and her left hand is at the ready to push the glasses in place, to not miss any academic steps. The class has started.

She is working with a small team on a math experience in which she is highly focused and looks like she is taking notes in a separate notebook. I wonder if those are her own private notes, and what she is collecting. There is a break in the class, so I head over to her desk and notice something dangling off her pencil case. "I'm not weird. I'm gifted"

"Hey there Lori. I wanted to wait till you were finished with your work before I spoke with you."

"That is an interesting saying, 'I'm not weird. I'm gifted.' Tell me more about it." *She seems to be taken off guard by my topic of conversation, but then immediately engages because it's her saying dangling off her pencil case. It means something to her.*

"I would think that my work would be all the evidence needed to explain it."

I flash a quick smile across my face at her response. Very true. Cheeky, but true.

"I think you know why I am here, so let's plunge in." *She smiles back with an expression like, 'I dare you.' Man, this student is confident. This will be fun.*

"I was wondering what that saying could mean with a math challenge like this, 'One eighth as a decimal.' Can you name what most people would say is a 'best wrong answer' to this?" *Without missing a beat, she jumps right into the explanation.*

"Sure, it's one eighth." *I smile. She is right. That is what most people answer with. She quickly goes on.*

"Best wrong answers are things like:
0.8
0.08
0.18
1.8

But really, the correct answer for 1/8 as a decimal is 0.125 or half of a quarter (0.25)."

I giggle a little, and tap the saying dangling off her case. She smiles back, pushing her glasses back on her face, ready for the real work to begin.

• • •

Mary

It is time to travel back to elementary school again to talk with Mary.

I sit across from Mary. Her long black hair falls onto her shoulders. She gives a quick toss of her hair and shoots that spunky smile toward me.

"You look happy today. What's happening in your world?"

"I just got a new puppy!"

"Really? That sounds like great fun. What size is the dog?"

She gives me a look that says, "I think I heard a math problem in that question."

"The dog is about this big." *She's uses her hands, shows me, then grabs a pencil and draws out a picture of the puppy. With the picture finished we look at its size.*

"I wonder how big it will be if it grows to be twice the size of this. Wow!"

"I need to find out, 'cause I want to tell my dad I figured it out! I know I can."

And just like that, Mary is off to discover something. She is a true Mathineer. I think back to when I first met her two years ago in kindergarten, and how she is now, as a second grader. She is full of curiosity and puts in great effort to learn.

● ● ●

Mike

We will stay in elementary school to meet Mike. He has a short stocky build and brown hair. I've been working with the students in his class on fractions.

"What does it mean to make half of something?" *Many students squirm in their seats and look side to side with their eyes, but suddenly Mike speaks up.*

"I know what half a sandwich is. Every day when my mom makes me lunch, she takes the whole sandwich and cuts it right down the middle."

"What happened when your mom made the cut?"

Thinking, he starts to shift around in his seat and grabs a piece of paper and folds it in half.

"Well I have two parts of one sandwich. But they aren't two whole pieces. It's just two that are each half of it."

"Can you show us more of what you mean Mike?"

"Ok. It's like this paper. If I fold it in the middle and then open it up again, I see two halves of the whole. But I can fold it again and get four parts of the whole as well."

He continues to show more to the class and soon all hands are working on their paper folding as well. I think to myself. He's got it!

• • •

RyAnn

Well, you're almost there. We have one student left; little RyAnn. She is quiet, small, and thin, with red, long hair, and fair skin.

"Good morning RyAnn! I was wondering if you can help me with something." *She looks at me, with her feet swinging back and forth under the table.*

"Ok."

"How's your cat?" *I know that if I break the ice with questions about her cat, she will warm up to me a little more.*

"Did your cat bring you any more gifts?" *Her cat is quite a mouser, and we usually can work some math around this topic.*

"Not lately. I think she caught them all."

"Oh, I see. Lucky for you, you won't have any more of those gifts." *She just kind of smiles shyly and stares again at the table.*

"So today I wanted to talk to you about a few different types of counting and ways to think about numbers. Is that ok?"

"Yes."

"When we look at these numbers to subtract, what happens?" *RyAnn's legs stop swinging and her body language gives away what her response will be before she begins.*

"I don't know. I don't know how . . . well, I'm not sure."
RyAnn gets quiet and seems to retreat inwardly. I know I have a few seconds.

"Well what if we look at it this way. Let's look at the distance between two numbers."

I give a math prompt and I start to ask her some target questions. RyAnn is successful when using counting strategies to increase conceptual understanding. She uses hands-on manipulatives and visuals that she can see and touch. When I ask her to subtract, she struggles, but when I change the question to a counting or distance question, she has huge success.

"I don't know."

"Remember to strengthen your thinking. Let's look at the distance from 9 to 16."

RyAnn has learned that if she waits long enough, someone will do it for her! I don't do that with my instructional strategies.

"Ok, I'll try."

The characteristics of the students are now conveyed, and I feel another reminder of the Quadrants should be emphasized again. Here are their plots and positions in the Quadrants.

Figure 2.1

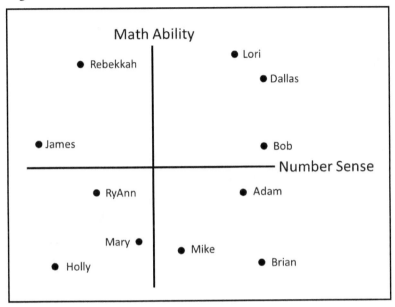

Many students like RyAnn need to be able to do some math independently. Showing them and doing it for them lets them off the hook. It is more efficient in the classroom to keep things moving, but we need to facilitate math connections, not just give our answers. If we continue to do it for them, children will continue to struggle to do it independently. I strive to ask a different target question, help them engage, and through their answers from the questions, I will know where to start again.

I hope this interview section has been powerful for you. I wanted you to meet the students and know who we will be working with throughout all the chapters. If at any time you need to come back and revisit anyone, feel free to see them in action here in Chapter 2.

3
TEACHERS—
CAN BE TAUGHT

WHAT IS IT that teachers do? I believe a teacher frames the student's mind, shapes language, and helps to influence the learning attitude of the students. Your job as a math teacher is no different. A teacher is not only a person who teaches various subjects, but also maintains discipline in a class.

A teacher helps to shape the structure and social rules of the classroom. They point out appropriate and inappropriate behaviors. Teachers are necessary to facilitate the learning experiences their students will have in order to learn new things in life. What is a classroom without a teacher? A place of chaos. Teachers make the magic happen.

Ok teachers, are you feeling the pressure? I know I did as a classroom teacher. Ethically and morally, I was ruled by the fact that I wanted my students to make progress, and sometimes they didn't. No matter how much effort I poured into prep time, the kids may not be consistently making any gains. In fact, it got to the point where I had to have a conversation with myself.

There has to be a way that I can impact more students and create a better experience for them, in which they will learn the information and retain it in the long term. But I didn't have any more time to spend on the planning.

Time! Time! I thought, *I can't get the results that I want. Look at all the time and effort I am putting in. I spend over 15 to 20 hours a week in prep time that I am not getting paid for, all in the hopes that I can make an impact for the students that they can demonstrate.* I remember thinking several times during my first two years of teaching that there was no way I could spend less time and get better results.

I was frustrated about putting in energy and not getting the outcomes I wanted from the students, whether through engagement, love of math, or their understanding of the content. After hours and hours of planning for a particular unit, I thought, *Forget it! I'm not even going to take the time to plan lessons anymore! I'm going to plan as little as possible and see what happens.*

Teachers let's have a heart to heart conversation right here while you are reading. Please raise your hand if you have had similar thoughts before. I am imagining nearly everyone's hands going up in the air. Hmm, I see. Ok, you may put your hands down. I want to show you that there are thousands of other teachers in your same position, and that you are not alone.

I didn't know it at the time, but it was the day the Achievement Formula came into existence that I had this shift in my thinking. The Achievement Formula is a lesson design and delivery process that allows teachers to teach more in less time with less planning and less stress. That is a topic for another day, but you will get the tip of the iceberg in this book and hunger for more!

I discovered my results were the same, whether I put in extra effort or not. That's simply not ok with me! I knew I had power over one thing—myself. From that day on, I *chose* to change the only thing I could, and that was me.

I engaged in some high-level professional development with a university professor and a cohort of urban teachers. I gained a huge change in perspective from that group, even though I taught in a suburban school. Mixing things up prompted me to do some action research in my own classroom. I asked myself, *how does the brain learn and retain information? What are the barriers to the brain as it tries to learn?*

As I spent more time in the research and in my own student action studies, I did less and less lesson planning. I needed to know how to capture my students and hold them where they could grasp concepts and move through the Quadrants from wherever they were initially plotted.

Deep breath. Side note: There is a tendency for teachers to fall into a mindset about students that *Kids don't get it or they don't care to get it.* When we have that mindset, we seem to trap ourselves in a place that no growth for them or us can happen. We have all been in a position where we were frustrated with the outcomes our students were achieving.

I think many of you reading this book take a lack of student learning personally. I know I did. I knew that if there was something to do differently, I was going to figure it out. There had to be a better way to help students experience math and improve. And when we know better, we do better.

> "Do the best you can until you know better. Then when you know better, do better."
>
> —Maya Angelou

It's time to learn who our teachers are.

Let's take a look at Jennifer. She shared the same story with me, even though we were in different classrooms, districts, and cities. We were both frustrated with kids who didn't do homework and parents who were not involved. I knew, as did Jennifer, that we couldn't control any of those factors. We couldn't spend our careers trying to change the system. All we could do was to give the kids in our stewardship the best educational and mathematical experiences possible. We needed to focus on our teacher instruction, which will give us control over student learning.

I discovered through the research that I must expose students to exploration, conversation, visualization, and representation, and to set expectations for them. We will dive deeper into this in Chapter 9. These are the actions I incorporated in my classroom. I did what worked for the students and tossed out what didn't. Suddenly I started seeing results.

I started to be questioned about my methods, by parents, then other teachers and administrators. And at first, I was upset with their questions. It seemed critical, and I was a little taken aback by the queries. I responded in some cases with, "How dare you question what I am doing! I am finally seeing these great results!" But I realized that I had misinterpreted the stakeholders' questions.

I thought they were accusatory, but truthfully, they were just curious! They wondered why Jonily's students were achieving more than other students. Administrators were, of course, extremely interested to know why practices that didn't fall in line with the current evaluation systems were getting such great results.

Through questioning my activities, they were genuinely asking for more understanding about what I was doing that made such a difference. At the time I honestly couldn't fully articulate my approach, or the growth I had experienced that had created such change. But once I was able to extract from my mind the evolution in my practices that enhanced student learning, I created an instructional design and delivery system called the Achievement Formula. I was able to replicate our growth through this framework, and help other teachers use the tools. Parents soon began to understand more, and administrators finally had a new way of looking at mathematical experiences in classrooms.

I'd like to introduce you to teachers willing to share their stories with you.

● ● ●

Jennifer is a rural secondary math teacher that has taught in several different schools over her 20-year career. Because she has been exposed to different administrations, teaching cohorts, and students, she feels that she is well rounded in her professional development and in her ability to reach students. With each move to a different school, she has made a lasting impact and spark, helping students come alive!

The feeling that she was truly impacting her students had diminished over time. As her 20th year of teaching rolled around, her ability to notice her impact had virtually disappeared. Occasionally she observed a few sparks of influence, but overall, it simply was not there. She found herself marking off the days until retirement. She thought, *the kids don't get it and don't want to get it.*

This was Jennifer's state of mind when she came to one of my professional development days. After spending a few hours in curriculum design, she began to feel the flame and the fire again. I saw her begin to shift and change because she saw the immediate difference in her students.

● ● ●

Jill teaches in a large Title 1 (Federal monies given to schools to support educational goals of the high percentage of low-income students) urban school. The students she teaches struggle with many things including behavior and academics. Some of her students have been in and out of juvenile detention.

She pours herself into her kids because she values each student and hopes to make an impact for at least one of them. She sees math as factual and wants students to acquire fact fluency. Jill feels that if the students put the time in to learn their math facts, they will be accelerated coming into the next year.

Fact fluency, or the math skills on the "just know these facts" list, are important for a variety of reasons, but facts are only one category of the four fluencies.

● ● ●

Amy teaches in a suburban Title I building. She was new to teaching only about three years ago. She has good math knowledge, but as a student she had been a proficient mimicker, meaning she always waited for an example to complete her work. She confesses that as a youngster, she *played school well.*

When it comes to math, she knows there must be better ways to teach it, but she is not exactly sure how. Amy has the heart to learn, and she was a great fit for the new project I was conducting at the time.

As a sixth-grade math teacher, she was asked to be part of a project to shift math instructional practices and evaluate the outcomes of student math learning based on the teaching methods. I provide training in the Achievement Formula, a system of instructional strategies, to the teachers. Then we follow the students as they grow and collect data. Amy feels a little beaten down by the traditional system and wants to rev up her internal drive in order to see her students have math success.

● ● ●

Liz teaches fifth grade in a suburban school district. She brings high quality—real class—to her teaching but struggles with helping the kids to fully understand math. Why? Because she personally hates math. She feels lost in the relationships and Number Sense of the math, based on her previous math experiences and limiting beliefs. She feels that in all her years of teaching, math has been a struggle. She can follow an example and plug things into an equation but is missing out on some bigger mathematical understanding.

She stays small in her math teaching to feel safe. She pushes facts, drills them, assigns worksheets, survives, and the students are able to get through it. But learning math skills doesn't entail merely surviving or getting through subject matter. As a result of her limited math approach over her 25 years of teaching, her students see no real gains while in her class.

• • •

Rachel is a second-grade veteran teacher of 20 years, working in suburban schools. She is doing all she can to set up her elementary kids with a good introduction to their math facts and procedures, so that they will have a foundation on which to build. Some things click and look like they are working, but she never wants to take them into deeper work. She allows her fear to limit her instruction. She is afraid the students will hit a proverbial wall, and crash and burn. If that happens, she will be left with a mess. No way! She does not want that.

• • •

Linda is a first-grade teacher who has been working in a suburban school for 15 years. She struggles with rigor and extending meaning. There are many opportunities to mentally stimulate cognitive thinking, but she is unsure where that type of thinking will lead the students. Linda is very similar to hundreds of teachers I have met over the years. She is quite linear in her thinking.

She likes to approach math in the same way. She feels that it makes sense for her to be safe. But what is comfortable for the teacher is not usually what's best for the student. Because of her mindset, Linda is missing the opportunity for growth with her students. Many of them could handle the rigor of extending mentally and cognitively to experience stimulating mathematics, but she is too afraid to take them to a place that will push their potential.

● ● ●

Karen has been an urban kindergarten teacher for 5 years, so she is newer in her career than others, and is open for ways to improve. As I observe Karen, I see that she is a great facilitator of math and a brilliant kindergarten teacher. She can facilitate a diverse group of students with many learning challenges. However, Karen limited their exposure to higher level (beyond kindergarten) math.

Karen struggles with keeping the student's attention and engagement. She does not know what to do with students who do not have prerequisite math skills. The bulk of her classroom consists of students with gaps in foundational math concepts, and other needs. There are a few students that are at a higher level, so she feels like she is being pulled in two directions by extremes of the ability spectrum. However, with the strategies I teach, Karen is able to meet the diverse needs of all the students and increase understanding, engagement, and independence in math learning.

● ● ●

Donald is a 4th grade teacher in a rural school district. He is soft spoken but has a striking impact and presence in his classroom. He is short to medium in build, with glasses. He is deeply reflective and articulate.

Generally, he asks thoughtful, open-ended questions during his instruction. He is well versed in growth mindset, and sets up his classroom with rich, open-ended math experiences. He has great pedagogy, but lacks math complexity, staying too long with one idea, instead of moving forward with urgency. My work with him allows him to gain depth in his teaching and increase the rigor with which he engages his students.

Teachers, I hope you have identified with some of these educators. I know that each one of you is highly unique, truly individual, and competent in your own teaching practices that no one can possibly duplicate. However, in showing you these examples I hope to build relationships of trust with you, and that you will invite me to your class to help you with your work as we continue *making Mathineers* together!

4
REBEKKAH—
WHERE IT ALL STARTED

HOW MANY OF you have been asked by your administrator/ principal to take a little field trip to find out where your students live? In my early years of teaching my principal would assign the teachers this task each year and it was very enlightening. Are you curious to know some of your students' living circumstances so that you can get to know them better? At the beginning of the school year and my first-year teaching, I eagerly looked forward to the Friday after-school drive to see where my students lived so that I could better prepare to understand their situations.

I finished grading the last of the math papers and glanced at the clock. School had been out for 40 minutes. I stacked the papers and tucked them into the folder, and with a few clicks shut down the computer. It was Friday and time to drive home, but on my way, I was going to take the assignment from my principal seriously and check out where my students lived. I had the list of addresses and quickly arranged them by location to save time and gas. I grabbed my purse, bag, and keys. I pulled my classroom door shut and locked it. "Bye," came the voice of a fellow teacher. "Bye. Have a good weekend," I replied.

As I pulled out of the school parking lot that unusually hot September afternoon, I wondered what I would find on this adventure. I headed south four blocks and came to my first apartment complex of the three I would drive past on my route today.

The first set of apartments were two-story, red-brick and looked like they had been given a fresh coat of army green paint on the eaves. All the doors were brown with black numbering hung above the peephole where I could see the addresses. There was a gas station on the corner and a fast-food restaurant kiddy-corner from that, but it was still in a good part of town. The apartments were small, maybe one-bedroom to two-bedroom at the most. I looked on my list of the students who lived here. There were two. I noted their names and the description of the building and pulled out of that complex, headed in a southwest direction.

Three blocks later I came to the second set of apartments. I set my blinker on, watched the oncoming traffic with caution, and safely made the left-hand turn into the complex. I slowly drove over the speed bump and parked in the guest parking area in front.

These were older looking apartments. They had a retro, 1960's shoebox-look to them: boxy with rectangular orthogonal shapes with regular horizontal rows of windows and paneled walls. There were also open-backed stairs and mid-century modern railings. A few children were out on the open patio tossing a ball back and forth and laughing at whatever game they had created. They reminded me that my time was running short, so I looked back at my list. One student lived here I noted, on the third floor.

I fired up my van again, reversed out of my space, put it into gear, and flashed my blinker to take me north out of the complex. Heading toward the edge of town, I noticed the houses were smaller, red-brick, two-bedroom homes all tucked together like little barracks from World War II. A couple of these apartments already had a few pumpkins and scarecrows on their porches, in anticipation of fall.

I drove past a few sets of duplexes intermingled among the small houses and wondered where the final apartment complex was. I looked at the address again. It should be coming up on my left soon. I followed the bend in the road which led to three complexes, all with different names and styles. I spotted the name Rose Oaks.

I circled the block once, making sure I had the right apartment complex of the three. I found a parking spot and turned off the van. Rose Oaks was brand new! The siding was a mixture of brown, red, and tan brick. I looked at the numbers B 17, C 23, and A 6. Three students lived here. I looked at Rebekkah's address—number C 23. Her apartment was off to the left, tucked back from the rest.

I started the van again and began to circle left around the apartment toward the exit. As I did, a flash of movement caught the corner of my eye. It was Rebekkah and her mom. Rebekkah's long hair was waving in the afternoon breeze and she was holding groceries. Mom held a cigarette in her left hand as she worked the key to the apartment door. The lock opened and the two slipped in, shutting the door just as I passed by. They never saw me. But the number C 23 burned into my mind. I would remember where they lived, and a little more about her. I looked forward to teaching her and the other children next week.

• • •

In class the next day, as all the kids filed in, I noticed Rebekkah's long hair was pulled up into a ponytail. It had been waving around in the wind yesterday. I watched her take her seat and get things ready to start the day. Her pencil dropped off the desk and she stretched out her leg to reach it with her foot and guide it back to her with pointed toe. She flipped it from her shoe and quickly grabbed it again. She was remarkably nimble and quick.

I quieted the class and asked everyone to look at the board. I had placed a math prompt on it. Many in the class put their heads down and started work on it. As some of the students became upset, she continued to work with her pencil in hand, going across the paper in the independent way she had about her. That made me smile. That was her *all business* look—when she was working on her assignments. She glanced at me as she pushed her glasses that had slipped down a little, back up her nose and smiled. She had the answer!

It was time for the students to share what they learned from the math prompt.

"Gather into your groups," I said. "Team leaders pick someone to go first." Quickly I heard the chatter begin and I walked about the room, going to different groups, listening to the conversations and the excitement of discoveries. I watched how some students clowned around to avoid work, others talked simply to hear themselves talk, and some like Rebekkah were quiet, though not due to shyness. She was especially determined to share what she knew.

As I listened in on her group again, I smiled at her gentle persistence as she explained her reasoning and conclusion for what she had discovered. Yes, this 5th grader might not have looked like a loud outspoken chatterbox, but she was one who shared what she knew, memorized the facts, and gave me what I needed to see from her. She was going somewhere. She was not going to be satisfied with mediocrity, I could clearly tell, and I couldn't wait to see where she would end up.

SYMPTOMS

MY STUDENT STRUGGLES WITH _____.
TEACHERS, FEEL FREE TO FILL IN THE BLANK.

5
POSITIVE-POSITIVE—QUADRANT I

LET'S REVIEW CHAPTER one about Math Ability and Number Sense. Math Ability is taught and influenced through language, culture, and school learning. I call it *school math*. Basically, what it means is, do students know procedures and facts? Number Sense is the ability that students have to understand quantity: bigger, smaller, less or more. (see Figure 5.1).

Figure 5.1

Number Sense basics:

- Understanding magnitude (how big or small, more or less)
- Recognizing relationships between single items and groups of items (*five* means one group of five items).
- Understanding symbols that represent quantities (5 is the symbol for the word *five*).
- Making number comparisons (13 is greater than 10, and three is half of six).
- Understanding the order of numbers in a list (1st, 2nd, 3rd, etc.)

Since the next four chapters explain each Quadrant, please review the coordinate plane and see that in Quadrant I, both Number Sense and Math Ability are found. This is the optimal place to which we would love to see all students progress.

Figure 5.2

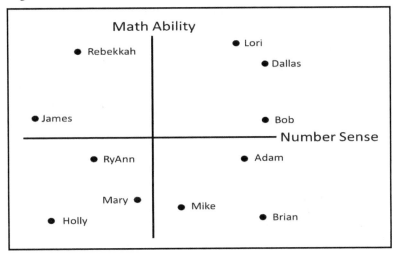

Now that we have gone through that quick refresher, I want to introduce you to a term that many states call *fluency*. The state of Ohio's fluency standard has three parts:

1) Accuracy
2) Flexibility
3) Efficiency

Many states have similar fluency standards. For math instruction, this is a good place to start, but to equip teachers to help students understand the math standards, we must categorize more specific types of fluencies. I have discovered in my 20 years of teaching, instructional coaching, and doing action research, there are actually *four fluencies*:

1) Procedural Fluency
2) Conceptual Fluency
3) Mental Fluency
4) Fact Fluency

The fluencies don't outrank each other, but each is needed for mathematical understanding. All four of these are absolutely essential to improve student outcomes. These fluencies also support Number Sense and Math Ability. (Warning: this might cause you some inner conflict within just a few paragraphs).

In *Making Mathineers,* it is crucial that teachers and administrators in schools know there are ways to not only improve the four fluencies, but to make significant gains in accuracy, flexibility, and efficiency. Alrighty then. Let's get to the four fluencies and discover what they mean.

Procedural Fluency is the ability to compute a math problem efficiently and accurately through a given procedure or algorithm. Fundamentally, a student should be able to look at a given problem and know the *school math* procedure to mimic it and solve it. There is not much of a need for flexibility. Procedures are important and have their place and purpose. However, if teachers tend to focus on practicing using the procedure over and over, their students will merely be mimicking the operation to *get the right answer*, rather than internalizing the number relationships.

Conceptual Fluency means to have *Number Sense*. Students understand the value and magnitude of numbers, and relationships between numbers. They can also comprehend the reasoning behind these relationships. Students appreciate the importance of accuracy of numbers. They are flexible in their approach to problem solving, and possess the efficiency required to complete the task. Students understand the *why* supporting a mathematical idea, including context, meaning, and conversation contained in the model. Students also know when a procedural fluency might be best for the types of numbers given.

Mental Fluency is the ability to think through and solve a problem efficiently and independently in your head. It takes flexibility and practice (multiple interactions over time) to increase mental Number Sense, visualization, and the ability to complete math problems. Mental fluency demonstrates math fluency. However, there is a warning with this! Many students can mimic the procedure up to a point in their heads, but conceptual fluency is needed for mental computation with large numbers.

For example, for the problems 4325 plus 1987, or 4325 minus 1987, students may use an algorithm and successfully find the answer in their head. This is not mental fluency because it will eventually expire. Large enough numbers will force a student to need paper and pencil for the algorithm because their brains can't retain the numbers in a stacked procedure, keeping the notation organized without losing accuracy. On the other hand, if a student thinks of the problem conceptually, by visualizing counting on a number line she can see the relationships and meaning, no matter the size of the number.

Fact Fluency, or in other words, *automaticity,* is the ability to recall answers to basic math facts or such as counting by 5's, 10's, single-digit addition facts, and single digit multiplication facts automatically and without hesitation. This is done by engaging in a variety of experiences and interactions over time, with the mastery of basic math facts being a goal of teachers, students, and parents. I call these the *just know* facts. The goal is to help kids get these facts down pat and increase Number Sense at the same time.

Well, that was nice and sweet: the four fluencies, presented in a neatly wrapped package.

But now I have a question for you. What does it mean to *polarize* something? It means to force something or someone to go in only one direction, or to divide into two very distinct groups. The two groups are grounded in belief. It's tough to dispute someone's belief. Something that is polarized may play on your moral conscience or fear.

Are you ready for a radical, messy, polarizing hot button topic to talk about? (I warned you a few paragraphs ago). For many in mathematics, the great and powerful *they*—people who talk about math, work in math, administrators, teachers, scared parents, congressmen, school boards, and even talk-show hosts have become *polarized* over two foundations of math, turning it into a war zone—the conflict between *procedural* versus *conceptual* math.

Individuals and organizations in these two mathematical camps each place great emphasis on either mimicking (procedural) or thinking and creating (conceptual) math. This battleground polarizes school boards and teachers to pick sides. Policies, school districts, teachers, administrators, and even legislatures with funding are all part of this battle. In the end, students are the casualties of this battle, and it is affecting generations.

As an instructional coach, I have been in hundreds of classrooms, and many are in this war zone, from rural to suburban to urban, low socio-economic, special education, and general student classrooms. I have also walked the halls of Title 1 schools as well as private schools.

There is a common theme I've found throughout my visits emanating from teachers and administrators. In these war zones they have expressed that they are fine if students simply know *procedures* without grasping *conceptual* components of math. The majority of parents feel the same way. Choke, spit, gasp! What? Why? The answer is simple! *Procedural fluency* is valued and understood more than conceptual fluency.

Consider the majority of school math systems that many were brought up in over the past 40 years. It was and still is based on *procedural fluency*. Occasionally one or two teachers in the entire school understood *conceptual math and* involved students in it prior to teaching them procedural methods. The reason so many have adopted procedural math learning is because it can be broken down into step by step instructions, whereas conceptual instruction is not a step by step process. It is more ambiguous. (Teachers I'll get back to you on this in Chapter 12).

Students who have been taught procedurally can complete problems and get the all-important right answers. Yes! My work is done, signed, sealed, and delivered! Teachers feel they don't have to describe theory because so many of their students are getting the answers correct.

But what just happened in the classroom? What do we teach and value? That the kids can mimic, plugin, get answers, receive praise and move on! But the bigger question is—move on to where? How many students are left behind with this focus—the ones with the capacity to think more analytically? Is this what we want?

Consider the sixth-grade students I recently worked with on division. They had no conceptual understanding of the operation, yet they could procedurally divide.

$6 \div 3 = 2$ $6 \div 2 = 3$ $3 \div 6 = ?$ $2 \div 6 = ?$	Here are some prompts: $6 \div 3 = 2$ $6 \div 2 = 3$ But when asked to perform: $3 \div 6 = ?$ many students were unable to respond. This is where procedures override conceptual thinking. A few got out their phones and came up with 0.5, but without paper, pencil, or phone they said 2. I asked: $2 \div 6 =$ and many said 3. A few said 0.5. Almost none could articulate the value correctly. It was time to get the cognitive thinking going, push pause on the procedural imitation, and enlist hands on paper folding and playing with visuals in order to stimulate thinking and facilitate comprehension of the concepts.

Instructionally, it is easy to teach *how* to do a procedure because it is broken down into steps. As teachers, we can take the steps to teach students the order, with sayings and songs which help them remember, and with facts. Using those steps, many students can mimic what is shown them. They are able to produce an outcome that is acceptable, and we can check off the box for that assignment or unit.

Warning! If this is the foundation of all our math instruction, we are setting students up for failure. This is especially true for our special needs populations (see Chapter

7 for more information). We do need to use explicit and direct instruction when teaching procedures, but not when navigating Number Sense. We must do the opposite of giving explicit instruction, which is questioning and prompting.

Students have different strengths and weaknesses, as demonstrated in the Quadrants. Once students are plotted, we as teachers need to take them through a mathematical process that focuses on the areas they need to improve. If we choose to only do procedures with students, we will not be helping them advance to better coordinates in their Quadrant, or to expand their skills to a more favorable Quadrant. In fact, students who are not increasing their conceptualization of math may hit a comprehension wall during their lives, possibly shattering their world by limiting their abilities to progress in careers or other pursuits.

There are cognitive tasks and structures that help students increase their capacity to think critically, which is essential for problem-solving, creation, and Mathineer-ing. These are not step-by-step *following-the-game-of-school* instructions. When we help students experience math, they understand the *why* and can willingly engage in a productive struggle, with the guidance of the teacher. (We will show you these strategies in Chapter 11). Less cognitively-challenging tasks such as step-by-step direction-following, simply teach the steps of procedures, without gifting students with the fulfillment experienced by conceptual learning.

The prompts and questions we ask during a math experience help increase student thinking and cognition. If there was a step-by-step way to facilitate cognitive work, then it would become procedural itself, but that is not what we want. We need to think of conceptual math as *chunking* strategies together so that the math experience builds on previous concepts. This is what the Achievement Formula does. It is an instructional delivery system. This book, *Making Mathineers* provides the general outline to help you understand the process, to truly see the clarity of where you can take your students.

The goal of mathematics is to learn how to think conceptually through a problem, then to explain the solution by exploring and performing procedures. Both conceptual and procedural fluencies are important. They are not battlegrounds or things to polarize people or groups. Conceptual, procedural, fact, and mental fluencies are all instrumental in supporting student learning.

Teachers, look at the four fluencies again:

1) Procedural Fluency
2) Conceptual Fluency
3) Mental Fluency
4) Fact Fluency

This is where the math war zone ends! No one needs to fight another. It's time to take a stand. Are you going to be a part of math fluency or not? Ha ha, just testing you to see if you recognized polarization with that question! I just harassed you into a camp, this time to pick the fluencies or not. See our tendency to polarize?

Let's look at a student again, this time focusing on Quadrant I: the positive, positive skill level.

• • •

Students in the positive, positive Quadrant have an innate understanding of *Number Sense* and *Math Ability*. They understand quantity, value, and magnitude, recognize relationships between single items and groups of items, and compare problems with solutions. They know which procedures to use, can explain the rationale behind them, and explain their thinking with visual representation. Never fear.

For the other students in your class, Number Sense is something that can be improved but it is *not* done through procedures and fact memorization. It is done through experiences. Warning! The following sentence can be terrifying to consider. For teachers, there are *not* step-by-step instructions to do experience-based math, so it can feel a little tricky. It may shake you a bit initially—trust me I know. But stick with me through chapters 5-8, and you will see what I mean.

Let's look back at one of our student's named Bob. We introduced you to him in Chapter 2. He loves math and reading. He enjoys playing and building with Legos. He likes to draw but believes he is not very good at it. He is a great thinker who enthusiastically shares ideas and participates in class. Dream student, right?

Bob is in Quadrant I. Bob needs to be mentally stimulated daily. We can do this by asking questions and giving prompts (target questions are taught in chapter 11). Target questions help us as teachers narrow in on what a student knows and doesn't know.

Bob's Math example

Count back by 10's from 62 How many halves make 24? How many three fourths in 24 wholes.	I asked Bob to count back by 10's from 62 (this is a target question). He responded: 52, 42, 32, 22, 12, 2, **-8**, -18, -28 etc. Bob didn't stop at 0. He knew there are numbers beyond 0. He kept going without much hesitation. He answered correctly, **-8,** which is rare for grade 2! Most common incorrect answers are 0, -2 and -12, once students say 2. I would say "best wrong answer". However, Bob didn't have any *best wrong answers*. He had the correct answers in second grade! I went on to ask him, "***How many halves make 24?***" Bob described it like this: "Each of the 24 things has 2 halves. You see, the number of things is doubled, so there are 48 halves in 24." He knew this without relying on paper folding (strategy in Chapter 11). When we did paper folding as a class, I had him figure out how many eighths in 24 wholes and ***how many three fourths in 24 wholes.*** He needed a challenge—to be mentally stimulated—so I gave it to him. Bob described finding how many eighths make 24 wholes like this: Well it is really a multiplication problem, 24 x 8, which I don't really know, but I could figure it out. Eight sets of twenty-five are 200, so it would be a little less than that. Bob continued to figure it out while I walked to another student, and when I checked back with him, he had finished correctly. I invited Bob on another experience to find how many three fourths there are in 24. This was tricky for him and he was still working on this as I wrote this part of the book.

Another way to challenge Quadrant I students daily is by asking questions that are variations of problems posed to all our students. Another powerful and clarifying activity we can have these students do is to create three of their own questions.

Bob came up with these questions:

1. How many two-eighths make 24 wholes?
2. How many one-fifths make 24 wholes?
3. How many two-fifths make 24 wholes?

Here is a side note: There are many students in grades 5-7 that give the *best wrong answer* of -2 for the previous prompt. These Target Questions and prompts help teachers identify which Quadrant students are in. *Best wrong answers* also help assess student placement in a Quadrant.

For students in 5th-7th grade I might also ask for the best wrong answer for the square root of 12. The best wrong answer for that target question is 6. Using the *best wrong answer* strategy improves conceptual understanding of the student and identification of Quadrant for the teacher.

Let's consider Lori again.

Lori is in 8th grade and a Quadrant I student. She was asked to show the value of 2^{-3}.

2^{-3}	Lori was able to show with paper folding the value of one section after the paper was folded in half three times. The negative in the exponent does not result in a negative number value, (which many students in middle and high school think) but it represents **division** by 2, three times, starting with 1 whole paper strip.
	Best wrong answers are -6, -8
	The correct answer is 1/8
	There are also many best wrong answers for the decimal equivalent for ⅛.
	Lori knows that this is 0.125 and can explain it as ½ of a quarter (0.25). Lori also knows the procedure for 1 divided by 8.
	Best wrong answers of high school students in Quadrant III (and sometimes Quadrant II and IV) for the decimal equivalent for 1/8 are 0.8 0.08 0.18 1.8 Among others

As you can see with our two examples, the positive, positive students understand math conceptually, can explain their math thinking, and perform the procedures. They truly have an innate understanding of numbers and challenging them with questions and prompts is a great game of skill and creativity.

*Side note: Teachers, no matter which Quadrants the students are in, you can still increase their Number Sense and their Math Ability with the strategies and target questions, which ultimately is the Achievement Formula. We are exposing only the tip of the iceberg in *Making Mathineers*.

6

FALSE-NEGATIVE—
QUADRANT IV

TIME TO LOOK at Quadrant number IV, the False-Negative. This is a positive-negative Quadrant.

Positive. What does positive mean in a Quadrant? This is the axis titled *Number Sense*.

I shared with you a study that John Hopkins did with children in Chapter 1. Let's take a look at some more research conducted by Dr. Elizabeth Brannon and Ariel Starr. With this research it was conducted with 48 babies who were around the age of 3.5 years of age. This research was supported by a National Institutes of Health grant R01 HD059108, a National Science Foundation Research and Evaluation on

> "When children are acquiring the symbolic system for representing numbers and learning about math in school, they're tapping into this primitive Number Sense."
>
> —Elizabeth Brannon, Ph.D.

Education in Science Engineering and Developmental and Learning Sciences Grant (Ariel Starr 2013).

Dr. Elizabeth Bannon wanted to prove that babies come into the world with a primitive, or a rudimentary understanding of *number*. We are not talking about the value of the symbol but the understanding that there is more or less of something. Dr. Brannon theorized that when babies look at two collections of objects, their primitive Number Sense allows them to identify which set is numerically larger even without verbal counting or using Arabic numerals.

For example, if someone looked at a group of 11 apples, they would be able to tell that it was more than 5 bananas just by glancing at it. When infants compared the apples and bananas, they were following similar patterns to the other study. If you can recall, the prior study was done by glancing at dots. The tests they conducted took 48 six-month-old infants to see whether they could recognize numerical changes. (Ariel Starr 2013)

They placed each of the babies in front of two screens: one that always showed the same number of bananas or apples (e.g. three), changing in size and position, and another that switched between two different numerical values (e.g., five and 18). All the arrangements of the fruit changed the size and the position. The researchers looked at how long each infant looked at the numerically changing screen.

Dr. Elizabeth Brannon's research was supported by Duke psychology and neuroscience graduate student Ariel Starr. Starr discussed that if we study how infants and young children conceptualize and understand numbers, it can lead to better mathematical instruction and strategies in school. "In particular, this knowledge can be used to design interventions for young children who have trouble learning mathematics symbols and basic methodologies." (Ariel Starr 2013) This is another foundational part of *The Achievement Formula*.

Following the infant testing, Brannon and Starr then tested the same children at three-and-a-half-years of age with a non-symbolic number comparison game. The children were again shown two different arrays on a screen and asked to choose which one had more dots without counting them. They were relying on their sense of primitive number— the Number Sense they are born with. In addition, the children took a standardized math test, scaled for preschoolers, as well as a standardized IQ test. Finally, the researchers gave the children a simple verbal task (asking 4-word sentences) to identify the largest number of words each child could concretely understand.

> In particular, this knowledge can be used to design interventions for young children who have trouble learning mathematics symbols and basic methodologies.
>
> —Brannon

"We found that infants with higher preference scores for looking at the numerically changing screen had better primitive Number Sense three years later, compared to those infants with lower scores," Starr said. "Likewise, children with higher scores in infancy performed better on standardized math tests." (Ariel Starr 2013)

Here is the challenge (which we touch on more in Chapter 8). Performance on the standardized math tests are more highly procedural in nature and are therefore more celebrated. Students who know how to mimic procedure and are good at learning facts seem to do well on the standardized math tests. This is why we have challenges in schools with a one-size-fits-all approach, or when we value procedural over conceptual fluency. Positive test results are short term and students tend to forget and must review often before exam day.

The strategies I teach in *Making Mathineers* include experiences needed to develop all four fluencies. It's not an either/or approach. They all are crucial. Students develop conceptual and procedural fluencies and that ends in positive test results. Students have also increased test results after an increased conceptual fluency without a strong procedural fluency. Basically, we can have our cake and eat it too!

Time to return back to the study. According to Brannon, the findings ". . . point to a real connection between symbolic math and quantitative abilities that are present in infancy before education takes hold and shapes our mathematical abilities." Does this sound similar to the John Hopkins study in chapter 1? Oh yes!

Brannon goes on to say, "Our study shows that infant Number Sense is a predictor of symbolic math. We believe that when children learn the meaning of number words and symbols, they're likely mapping those meanings onto pre-verbal representations of number that they already have in infancy," she said. (Ariel Starr 2013).

Something important to note—Even with research like this, no one can measure a baby's Number Sense and predict how they will do in math class or even on their SAT's. According to Brannon, the infant task study only explains a small percentage of the variance in young children's math performance. "But our findings suggest that there is cognitive overlap between primitive Number Sense and symbolic math. These are fundamental building blocks" (Ariel Starr 2013).

Let's dive into the Positive-Negative Quadrant number IV. On the positive side, these students have innate ability with their Number Sense as was shown in the study. On the negative side, they struggle with procedural fluency and fact fluency. I call these students false negatives because without the procedural fluency, teachers perceive them as "math strugglers." However, these students have great conceptual understanding.

Teachers can use the instructional strategies in this book to extract the conceptual understanding to discover that these students know more math than they thought. Once teachers have extracted the conceptual understanding, they can connect it to the procedural, symbolic and notational mathematics fairly quickly. Let's check these guys out. They are a fun group.

Here is something to help demonstrate the struggle that Positive-Negative students have. For example, how do we read words on a page? From left to right, right? I mean, correct? We have been trained in western culture that we read left to right, back and forth and in a downward loop until the page is read. It makes sense. But look at procedural math. Think about the algorithm for addition and multiplication. Have you thought about where it starts and how it ends? It is done right to left.

Suddenly we are stacking numbers on top of each other and changing directions going in a completely different direction from reading. We are teaching kids to go from right to left, managing the ones digit first. This can challenge anyone's mind and thinking through the steps of an algorithm can throw off the math as students try to apply it. Let's look at a procedure that matches the left to right thinking. If we add 40+40+40 first, we get 120. Then we can add the 4+4+4 and get 12. Finally, when we add together the 120 and 12, we get 132.

$$
\begin{array}{r}
44 \\
44 \\
+\ \underline{44} \\
120 \\
+\ \underline{12} \\
132
\end{array}
$$

Remember Brian from Chapter 2? We were introduced to him as one who was having a bit of a rough start and a challenging home life. He has a strong innate sense of number but struggles with Math Ability—school math.

When Brian was working on a math task, this problem came up. 44 + 44 + 44. He reasoned out the following in his head:

Math problem	Brian's innate thinking:
44 44 + <u>44</u> 44 + 44 + 44 =	He reasoned in his head 40 +40 + 40 is 120 (or 12 tens). He did not stack—that is procedural. He knew that 4 + 4 + 4 was leftover to combine. He knew that this was 12 (or 1 ten 2). He knew that 120 + 12 was 132. In other words, 12 tens + 1 ten 2 is 13 tens 2 is 132 He could explain the quantity through his conceptual understanding.

However, this is what happened when he did the same problem as a procedure:

| 44
44
+ <u>44</u>
1212 | When he used a procedure like stacking, he got 1212.

How? 4+ 4 + 4 = 12
And 4 + 4+ 4 = 12, Therefore you have 1212. |

The problems started showing up when we asked Brian to plug the numbers into an algorithm, or in other words, stack them vertically. When he did that, he got 1212. Wait. What? How? He didn't have an understanding of the procedural side of math to help him pass the school math. With our False Negative kiddos, we look at the strength of their Number Sense, so we know how to break down the Math Ability portion and help them complete the problem correctly.

Teachers often think that students like Brian struggle mathematically, but with these Quadrant IV students we need to extract their conceptual understanding of number (which they have but is hidden if our instruction doesn't look for it) and connect this to how the traditional algorithms work. These students are False Positive because we think they know less math than they actually do.

Let's take a look at Adam. He, too, was in this Quadrant. I met him while he was in kindergarten. He had a great smile and a cute chunky face, wore glasses, was short and quiet, but was unique and interesting when he shared what he was thinking. He was sweet and gentle, and wow—did he love life! He lived each moment to the fullest. That is a gift! Working with the Achievement Formula, Adam was able to move closer to Quadrant I.

Adam needed the opportunity to share his thoughts verbally. With promptings like, "What do you see?" "What do you notice?" and "Tell me about…", I was able to extract his hidden Number Sense. I could see what was lacking, and that he needed connections from his conceptual perspective to procedural and notational (with symbols) mathematics.

Adam and the other students in his class were given a Reference Task called the *Staircase*. A Reference Task is a math task that students engage with and experience, often throughout a school year and from one school year to the next. There are phases of implementation of the task, and students experience many interactions over time, gaining great mathematical depth for the math concepts and skills the tasks provide.

Reference Tasks are timeless, meaning that they connect to a variety of math standards at all grade levels, and the tasks don't expire at a certain point. There is always another layer of mathematics that can be uncovered, referenced, and connected to over time. Here is a breakdown of the task and a picture of what students are shown.

Staircase Problem Introduction	Students from kindergarten through high school have seen the staircase problem. On the first interaction with the problem I ask: **What do you see?** **What do you notice?** Or I might prompt: **Tell me about the pattern.** Students typically respond with: *I see a pattern.* *I see red blocks.* *It's getting taller.* *I notice that the height of the staircase is the same as the stage number.* *The pattern gets taller and longer.* *The length matches the stage number.* *The length matches the height.*
What math questions can you create?	On the second interaction I ask: **What math questions can you create?** The students create questions. For example: How many blocks make stage 8? How many blocks are needed for stage 10? Are there twice as many blocks in stage 10 as stage 5? Adam and his class began this process of being exposed to the Staircase Problem in kindergarten with the previous interactions. Using blocks to build stairs, Adam tried to figure out how many blocks were needed to make each stage, but he was counting the blocks by ones. I prompted him to try counting in chunks (more than one block at a time, strategically) to keep track, and so it wouldn't take so long. He wasn't impressed with my suggestion, so I didn't push the strategy. Part of the purpose of a Reference Task is to have students make sense and discover, *not solve*. Since the task is referenced many times, the students don't have to figure everything out with the task all at once. It's okay to leave some ideas unfinished.

Staircase stage 8	In first grade, Adam and his class were given the Staircase task. They were again focusing on stage 8.
Breakdown of the thinking.	The students noticed that to find the total number of blocks needed to build a certain stage number, you needed to add numbers together "next to" each other. (Student's would say "next to"). For example, for stage 8 the staircase was 8 blocks tall so you needed to add 8 + 7 + 6 + 5 + 4 + 3 + 2 + 1.
	Adam quickly said that is what he saw last year! I also reminded him that I wanted him to count the numbers in chunks instead of by ones.
	Even though the students were in first grade, I used the phrase "consecutive whole numbers" to be specific. I embedded math vocabulary by using the term "consecutive" to replace the student phrase "next to."
	This was a great time for me as the teacher to use this Reference Task as a teaching tool.
How do you add consecutive whole numbers efficiently?	***How do you add consecutive whole numbers efficiently?*** Students wanted to add 8 and 7 to get 15 (or 1 ten 5) and then add 6, etc.... However, I knew there was a more efficient way.
	Instead of just teaching a procedure, I asked the following questions.
What do you notice about stage 8?	***How can we visually represent stage 8 in a way that helps us count the total number of blocks efficiently? What do you notice about stage 8?***
What do you notice?	Adam quickly noticed that if you split the stage in the middle, you could see two stage 4's and a 4 by 4 square. Wow! I couldn't believe what he noticed! That is the beauty of asking the question ***what do you notice*** to get the student's perspective of the mathematics.

Below is the picture of how Adam saw the two stage 4's and a 4 by 4 square.

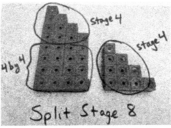

Adam said that we could make a rectangle with the pieces. I had him show me and I was amazed! I have presented this task dozens of times to a variety of grade levels and this was the first time a student had this perspective.

It was Adam, a Quadrant IV kid, in first grade. I now call this the "Adam split and rotate" strategy. The class was excited to learn from Adam and I was able to take his conceptual understanding and connect it to procedural math.

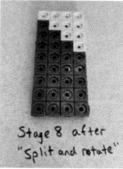

Stage 8 after
"Split and rotate"

8 + 7 + 6 + 5 + 4 + 3 + 2 + 1 became a rectangle that was 9 units tall and 4 units long.

I asked the question:
How do the height and length of the rectangle relate to the stage number?
The purpose of this question was to spark thinking, not for students to answer. If a student did give an answer, I would not confirm or deny the accuracy. As soon as I confirm or deny, the math thinking stops for everyone. This is another question I leave unanswered on purpose.

What students did notice was that there were these addition problems:
In the first column it is 8 + 1
In the next column it is 7 + 2
Then 6 + 3
And finally, 5 + 4

	There are 4 sums, and a student noticed that each of the sums is 9.
	And we have a rectangle that is a 4 by 9. We have an array of 4 columns with 9 rows.
	Adam could not necessarily come up with this concept or discover all this on his own, but that's the point.
	I listened to his conceptual reasoning (splitting and rotating it visually) and then my mini lesson was connecting the mathematical language, notation, and strategies.
	Adam needed to see this visual image (the blocks) connected to mathematical notations and symbols.
How does the height and length of the rectangle relate to the stage number? Exposure is just as important (if not more important) as Mastery.	I was not concerned whether Adam or other students mastered this strategy because Reference Tasks are used to *expose math concepts and skills*. Exposure is just as important (if not more important) as Mastery. Mastery happens with many exposures and interactions over time. There would be plenty more interactions for students to Master the mathematics.

69

Third interaction with the concept of Stairs:

Stage 12 How many blocks would be needed to make stage 12?	During the third interaction, I asked the class: **How many blocks would be needed to make stage 12?** Without any other prompting, one student said that we could use Adam's strategy and I let her explain the strategy. She explained beautifully that we could split stage 12 into 2 parts. She made sure to say that the parts were not halves because they are not equal.
	Another student then said that we could make a rectangle and Adam said that we could add together the lowest and highest numbers. 12 + 1 11 + 2 10 + 3 9 + 4 8 + 5 7 + 6 Adam was trying to chunk sets in the pattern so that he could count the number of blocks in each chunk and add those numbers together. Brilliant!
	He still struggled a bit with the adding, but he was conceptually able to see the most efficient way to count. By looking at the pattern he was able to see that he should get 13 for all of the answers (sums).
	This is a very deep math concept, but Adam, a somewhat struggling math student, was able to lead us down this path which led to helping find sums of numbers and increase fluency.

During the fourth interaction, Adam tried to count how many blocks were in stage 16, and if it related to stage 8. He noticed something truly amazing as he was playing and exploring.

How many blocks are in stage 16?	**How many blocks are in stage 16?** He said that if you split stage 16 into 2 parts (not technically in half because each part would have to be the same) then you have two stage eights and an 8 by 8 square.
	He also reminded us that with a stage 12 you could split and get two stage sixes and a 6 by 6 square.
	By this point all students were able to see this relationship and some students pointed out that 8 is half of 16 and 6 is half of 12.
How does the number of blocks in stage 16 relate to the number of blocks stage 8?	I helped the class interact with conversation that sparked more thinking. **How does the number of blocks in stage 16 relate to the number of blocks stage 8?**
	Although the class did not figure out the relationship between the number of blocks in stage 16 and in stage 8, great mathematical engagement and discussion happened.
What would the dimensions of the rectangle be, after a 'split and rotate' if we started with stage 20?	I closed the lesson with this question: **What would the dimensions of the rectangle be, after a 'split and rotate' if we started with stage 20?**
	I left that question unanswered and ended math time.
	The strategy of leaving problems and questions unsolved and unanswered is called *Salt*.
	It comes from the quote: "You can lead a horse to water, but you can't make it drink." I say, "You can lead students to learning, but you can't make them learn.
How will this lesson make students thirsty for learning?	You can give a horse a salt lick and then it will drink." When I plan math lessons, I ask myself the question: **How will this lesson make students thirsty for learning?** And I create a question, situation or prompt that I call *Salt* that will not be finalized but left lingering so that students continue to think!

71

Teachers, can you see their thinking? Can you see what they are working through and trying to solve? Do you see how conceptual and procedural math are working together and not against each other?

I try not interrupt their flow of thinking. Adam and the rest of the students were curious to see what would happen for any stage number. They did not mention any *odd stage number* and I didn't throw that in. (On a later interaction with this same task I would push to that level, but they got here because of what they were experiencing).

Connection	Another student in the class, a Quadrant II kiddo, who had okay conceptual thinking, but was more skilled with procedural thinking, showed me the steps to figure out how many blocks were in stage 8.
how many blocks?	"If we split the stage 8 and put the stage 4 on top then it makes a rectangle and we can use our 120 chart to figure out how many blocks!"
	We have used the 120 chart to skip count many times and she noticed that the rectangle would be 4 long (4 towers since we split the stage 8) and 9 tall.
	Then the student suggested we could either skip count by 4, nine times or skip count by 9, four times. With that idea in her head, she went to figure it out, as did others.
	I had not planned to interact with the Staircase task that day, but she was excited to share her discovery.

I asked some follow up questions with Adam and the rest of the class that I didn't expect students to be able to answer. I hoped to provide more exposure without an expectation of mastery. It is essential to push student thinking in a relaxed way. The students don't have to solve or figure out everything, but *they can continue to explore and think about* it.

Exposure is a low stress/low anxiety place for most students to be because there is no pressure to solve. There is only time to think and explore. This is how and when the magic of becoming a Mathineer takes place.

How do 4 and 9 relate to 8?	I wrapped up the impromptu conversation with these questions:
	When we split and rotate stage 8 we end up with 4 towers that are 9 high, **how do 4 and 9 relate to 8?**
What if we did the 'split and rotate' strategy with stage 10? Or with stage 14?	**What if we did the 'split and rotate' strategy with stage 10?** **Or with stage 14?**
	The students will continue to think about the answers to these questions!

Let's take a look at Mike. Mike was a cute little character. His brown hair was spiked a little, but I'm not sure if that was on purpose, or because he was running out the door to get to school and didn't have time to comb it out or work on it. His round face always greeted me with a smile and he truly wanted to learn. Mike was an interesting student when it came to math.

*Side note: Teachers, there will be students you will run into that are similar to Mike. These students have good conceptual understanding, and at times will have good procedural thinking; *however*, they still have gaps to fill and will struggle. It takes a savvy teacher and informal assessment practices to extract the knowledge of all students, Like Mike, they may appear to understand the mathematics, but then with formal assessment fall short. Be on your toes and don't assume that all is well.

Before asking students to solve the problem 476 ÷ 7, I would ask them to make sense of this situation. This instructional strategy is essential in building conceptual understanding. There are many responses students give to provide evidence of their sense making:

> *There are 476 envelopes and 7 boxes to put the envelopes in.*

> *If we skip count by 7, how many counts will it take to get to 476?*

> *This could be a rectangle with an area of 476 square inches and height of 7 inches.*

These responses are based on students having conceptual experiences for division.

I asked Mike this math question in 4th grade:

| 476 ÷ 7

 A bar model is a rectangle drawn on paper to represent the paper strip from paper folding. The bar model is a visual representation for division, fraction, and other concepts. The bar model is sometimes called a tape diagram. The bar model can be used as a visual representation as a double line and a number line. | Procedurally we would do a long division process, but Mike and some other students couldn't get through it efficiently or accurately. (remember chapter 5).

 Mike and students like him have a strength in flexibility - what I mean by this is they are able to reason through the computation by breaking numbers apart and putting them back together.

 Instructionally, I use the Bar Model to visually portray the thinking.

 The entire rectangle/bar represents a value of 476 and the bar can be split into sections to help visualize the division process and connect to Mike's thinking. |

Remember, we are focusing on Mike's strengths: his keen sense of conceptual thinking. We use that strength to formalize his thinking and eventually connect it with procedure.

Here is the next question.

What number less than 476 is divisible by 7?	**What number less than 476 is divisible by 7?** Students say things like 14, 21, etc.
	Mike said 70. This was a great starting place! Quadrant I students say 420 which is beautiful. We can't expect other Quadrant kids to come up with that, but we want to move them closer to it.
	I hope readers see the beauty in all that is happening here!
	I prompt the students with this:
	The area inside the rectangle must be 476 square inches and the height is 7 inches. Why?

Teachers, we want to use Mike's strong Number Sense to solve. This strategy can also increase Number Sense for students who are weak in that area. I must caution to not use the Bar Model in a procedural way because then we defeat the purpose of connecting the algorithm from the conceptual understanding.

For example, I could guide students explicitly, step-by-step, through what to do next and next and next, but that would be improving procedure, which is fine, but not the goal. I see this again and again in classrooms. We use a great strategy to tap into conceptual understanding and then we proceduralize it. There is nothing wrong with teaching procedures. However, It is an issue if it isn't the goal, and if what we want is to improve or connect more fully to the conceptual.

Part of the Bar/ Rectangle is now 70.	So, Mike and I started with 70.
	I recommended that another part of the bar be 6, but Mike didn't like that I didn't either. But it would help us continue to reason and think. This number is tricky to break down, especially for non-Quadrant I students.
From 476 we have 406 left to deal with.	
	I have to say that I do not typically start with a trivial example, $77 \div 7$. It is most beneficial to begin with something a bit complex but within reach.
	Remember, students *are not* expected to answer this independently at this point.
What is another number, greater than 70 but smaller than 400 divisible by 7?	We have separated 70 and 6 and now I ask: **What is another number, greater than 70 but smaller than 400 divisible by 7?**

Why do I ask this? Because I want students to *think in chunks*. Counting is essential, and that is what we do with division—we count. Efficient counting is the goal. The strategy for this goal is to count in chunks—we have 70 and 6. Remember we don't like 6 but we are going to leave it and see what happens.

We need a number between 70 and 400 to figure out the next section of our bar.	Mike did not say 350 as I would have liked; he said 140.

I prompted "higher" he struggled a bit but then we listed 70, 140, 210, 280, 350, 420, 490.

I asked one of my favorite questions: **What do you notice?**

Mike noticed that these are "regular multiples of 7 but ten more."

I dug a little deeper at the phrase "10 more."

I said, "Tell me what you mean by 10 more," and he said that each ends with zero, so there are no one's, but the other two digits are multiples of 7, to which you can multiply ten.

I responded that these are all multiples of *7 and 10* but written such that the ten and hundred digits together are clearly the multiples of 7 (with a zero in the one's place – which makes it a multiple of 10). We see this on the 120 chart, because there are other multiples of 7 not like this. |

I extend the question a bit and asked for other multiples of 7 that are not also multiples of 10, and why we wouldn't use them for this strategy.

How much is left from 476?	We have a section of 70, one of 6, and one of 350, for a total of 426. So how much is left from 476?
	Mike noticed right away that 50 was left; we could put it in with the 6 to make 56.
	Because he knows 7 times 8 is 56, and that will help us.
	Students in Quadrant III who doesn't yet know that 7 x 8 is 56, will not think about putting the 50 with the 6.
	So, with a Quadrant III student, I would put the 50 aside and pull another number divisible by 7 but less than 50, to target a fact that a struggling student may know. We can also have a multiplication chart available if needed.
	With Mike we have 350 and 70 and 56.
	That tells us that the length of the rectangle is 50 and 10 and 8 which is 68.

I want to point out that our goal here is *not* for students to learn a procedure or to be efficient. The goal in showing you this is to *improve conceptual understanding, Number Sense, flexibility, and reasoning*. Why? So that this math experience can be eventually connected to the long division procedure algorithm. Both the conceptual and procedural are important, and never is one above the other.

7
QUADRANT III—
NEGATIVE-NEGATIVE

QUADRANT III: NEGATIVE, negative student. This must sound like a terrible name. This is not directly labeling a student but identifying a mathematical struggle. Growth mindset people should not freak out. We are using these Quadrants for teacher instructional purposes. Students are already aware of their weaknesses, and by helping them with conceptual instruction, they will feel more successful. We help fill their gaps, they gain more understanding, they grow, and become more confident.

Giving students math experiences is how we teach growth mindset and nurture their success. It doesn't happen by merely telling them about math. Students in this Quadrant have weak Number Sense and weak Math Ability. For children in this Quadrant, we as teachers need to be aware of one big idea. Weakness in two areas doesn't mean it is hopeless; building math sense and capability is absolutely possible.

I have two sayings that I use during any teaching experience with the students:

1. I don't teach math; I teach thinking.
2. Show me your best wrong answer.

"I don't teach math; I teach thinking." What is implied in the meaning of that sentence to students? Many students will ask me, when referring to math, "When will we ever use this?" I respond with, "Thinking? Probably never." Some of them catch the irony, and others give me a blank

> "I don't teach math; I teach thinking."
>
> —Jonily Zupancic

stare. I quickly toss in a reassuring smile, hold their hand, and dive into the thinking with them. Thinking is the way to solve challenges and problems, so that is what we are doing with our students, through experiences.

I want students to show me how they are thinking. If they know it is safe to expose their weaknesses, that they can trust me to not mock or scold them for their answer, they are more willing to go through the thinking process to find the answer.

Teachers, here is one more thing to think about since we are in Quadrant III: Exposure vs. Mastery. Too often math teachers teach for mastery only. This means that students are not exposed to higher level math concepts. We think they can't possibly understand something that is going to be more complex, because we've become used to the concept that what we teach must be mastered. Here is the truth, *not every problem or stimulus we show kids has to be a topic or skill that they master.* I know, I know! Shocked right? You can close your gaping mouth now.

This is important to understand because if we don't expose them to higher levels, we narrow the content we give kids, thinking that if we teach it, we have to test it; but that is just not true. By exposing students conceptually to above-grade-level math content, they get more interactions over time, and that is exactly what Quadrant III students desperately need.

Let's break down the math symptoms that students in Quadrant III present within the classroom. I'm sure many of you can identify these before I do. Here is a quick and dirty list of them:

- Low motivation caused by math anxiety
- Lack of positive math experiences and low math successes
- Lack of an innate grasp of numbers
- Poor working memory
- Poor math-fact recall and automaticity
- Poor understanding of simple number concepts
- Difficulty learning number facts and procedures
- Difficulty estimating numbers
- Learning disabilities
- Dyscalculia

As an instructional coach across all grade levels, I wanted to show preschool through secondary school teachers student symptoms specific to grade. This is not a comprehensive list, but it breaks things down for the purposes of this book.

Preschool teachers often see student math symptoms such as:

1. Difficulty learning how to count.
2. Trouble connecting number values one-to-one with an object or group of things, such as 4 bears, 4 apples or 4 friends.
3. Struggling to recognize patterns and comparisons, such as smallest to biggest or shortest to tallest.

Math symptoms of elementary math students in Quadrant III:

1. Difficulty with working memory in order to recall basic number facts and relationships with numbers.
2. Stuck in non-efficient counting strategies—counting by ones and not in more advanced strategies such as counting in chunks, groups, or sets.
3. Struggling with remembering operational signs, such as + and -, when to use them and what they mean.
4. Failing to recognize that addition and multiplication are commutative: 3+4 gives the same result as 4+3. Whereas, subtraction and division are not commutative. Changing the order of the number changes the answer.
5. Difficulty with place value and *stacking numbers* according to a procedure.
6. Struggling to understand and apply math vocabulary.
7. Difficulty keeping score in a game.
8. Mimicking but not understanding things like money, time, and measurement.

Improving Number Sense at the secondary level is not employed as an intervention program. It is expected that regular instruction connected to grade level and course content will suffice. But students should not be expected to have Number Sense when entering high school. Some will and some won't, and it is our responsibility to continue to improve student conceptual understanding of numbers throughout secondary math.

The study done by Johns Hopkins University also states that Number Sense does not peak until we are 30 years old, unlike other cognitive processes and skills that peak around 18-21 years. I believe this results from not valuing or correctly defining Number Sense from preschool to graduation, and we not instructing in or offering math experiences that target improvement of Number Sense. Therefore, students lack the experiences they need in math class to allow Number Sense to peak earlier.

What happens in secondary education if all of these foundations are not filled in? Teachers in secondary school see the math symptoms of their students as:

1. Difficulty comprehending information on charts and graphs.
2. Struggling with facts, fractions, and equation solving.
3. Lacking flexibility with application.
4. Inability to mimic well.
5. Following procedures and completing algorithms is challenging.
6. Deficiency in working through multi-step problems independently.
7. Lacking confidence in individual math abilities.
8. Struggling with fractions, decimals and percentages.

Please note that it's never too late to improve Number Sense. It is best to start as early as possible to develop Math Ability and conceptual understanding, yet we can help them improve while teaching grade level content.

I have a teaching that I call the 3 M's: Mistakes, Misunderstandings, Misconceptions, and I try to make sure that I am using these words in context. The 3 M's are a way to evaluate student errors and inaccuracies.

Mistakes are errors that students can typically correct on their own, seeing what the teacher has pointed out or marked incorrect. Students can correct these without instruction.

For example, a student answered with the number 54 for the equation 8 x 7, when asked to correct said, "Obviously!"

and was able to correct to 56 quickly and without much thought.

Misunderstandings are errors students make that need a bit of teacher instruction to correct. I always use the TV show *Three's Company* as the example of this—I know this dates me! On the sitcom, everyone had misunderstandings throughout the episode, but the audience knew the whole story and would think, "Gosh, if they just knew this *one* thing there would be no more confusion!" And that's what I see in math.

If this student simply knew this *one thing*, they would fill the "misunderstanding gap." What is the *one thing*? The *one thing* needs to be facilitated by the teacher, as the student will typically not discover the *one thing* on his own.

For example, with the subtraction problem $2 - 6$, a student might look at it and say, "I can't do it." I would prompt, "Yes you can. What do you think the result will be?" Many students may think about a number line and travel the distance. They would find 2 and start to count back. They may say, "It's a negative number!" I know this might be hard to believe but many of our elementary kiddos have much more understanding of things than we think – hidden understandings.

We need to challenge ourselves with effective instructional practices described in this book to uncover as much student math conceptual perspective as possible. Students in elementary school are exposed to this all the time when they are following stacking subtraction procedures with regrouping (32-26 or 92-48) and we need to take advantage of discussions that will extract their understandings and misunderstandings. When kids are given an opportunity to show their perspective, it's amazing what we can unpack and use to increase their overall math sense.

Misconceptions errors that students make show gaps in math understanding that require a significant amount of facilitated experience by an expert teacher or math specialist trained with strategies and techniques to fill these student math gaps. Students in Quadrant III have many misconceptions because they don't have innate Number Sense and they have weak Math Ability. These students may not even be aware that a negative number is a possibility for 2 − 6. Therefore, negative numbers would not be used to think flexibly about subtraction problems such as 32-26 or 92-48.

When there are educational discussions about students doing test corrections, I say, yes, this is appropriate if the errors are mistakes. If the errors are misunderstandings or misconceptions, then having the student do test corrections *will not fill* their achievement gap. They need further instruction by the teacher. By the way, I don't have much of an opinion on some of these hot topics, such as retakes, test corrections, timed tests, use of calculators, and so forth, because I have a love/hate relationship with these ideas.

I love it when they are used appropriately—when the students have a warm outcome. I hate them when they are used poorly or are attached to the wrong goals. We tend to spend too much time debating these topics and ignoring how and why they are used in certain situations.

Let's talk about timed tests. My first question is "What is the goal?" If the goal is to assess speed and accuracy, that matches the exercise. Some students thrive on timed tests. Quadrant II students love them and Quadrant I students do well on them but don't necessarily love them. We could take them or leave them because we know what they know and keep assessing them anyway.

It's kind of like poking the pig; it will eventually get annoyed. Quadrant III students will get annoyed when they are continuously assessed with timed tests and have poor results. Quadrant II students may be motivated and thrive on timed tests because this is their strength. They do well on this type of assessment and want to show that they do well.

It's a positive, motivating experience for these kids. But no students want to have the same experiences every day.

Now let's think about Quadrant IV students and timed tests - these kids may not typically do well, but they are a mixed bunch. They have accuracy but need a bit more time than is often allowed. If I already know this, I don't need to give them this assessment tool. I need to focus on the instruction to improve fact fluency, not a timed test. A timed test is an assessment, not instruction.

If I don't know these kid's skills, a timed test might be appropriate. At the buzzer I hand out different colored pens and give them more time to complete the problems. This allows me to see what they knew quickly with the first color, and what they knew conceptually with the second color—a 2-dimensional assessment. Timed tests will assess speed, accuracy, and automaticity but will not necessarily assess efficiency or flexibility. Just know your goal when you give an assessment and make sure your students know the goal.

Now Quadrant III students don't need a timed test to tell me what I already know, that they are not going to do well. They know they are not going to do well and may be anxious. It doesn't make sense to place them in a position of probable defeat. It's important to nurture confidence by giving students many experiences that will help them feel successful, rather than intentionally showcasing their weaknesses and beating them down.

Students in Quadrant III need experiences with math in order to improve their Number Sense and their Math Ability. Even students that have been given the diagnosis of dyscalculia can improve their skills through math experiences.

We need to start where kids are, find their strengths, and connect them to their deficiencies in a way that will move them toward Quadrant I to the conceptual. I have seen it work brilliantly with students who begin deep in Quadrant III, yet continue to make gains. In my next book, I am going to take you on a deep and thorough examination of dyscalculia. I can't wait; but for now, I am going to share more of what I do for students who are in Quadrant III.

• • •

Holly was a student I met while coaching a teacher. Holly is average size and build for her age, with long blonde hair. She is quiet in class but very outspoken in non-class setting like lunch and recess, with spunk rarely seen during class. She didn't appear to care much for math and seemed like she was just trying to get through it. She struggled with focus, follow through, initiative, and stamina.

The teacher actually wanted me to work with Holly so that I could share the formula or trick the teacher needed in order to work with her successfully. It wasn't simply one trick or tip that she needed. I had to show the teacher, as well as Holly, that through the experiences we provided, she could increase her Number Sense and Math Ability. She was like many of the students I meet who operate in Quadrant III. The teacher easily identified her weaknesses:

1. Telling time.
2. Placing a number value to money.
3. Stacking numbers to add or subtract.
4. Math facts.

I needed to know which Quadrant Holly was in so I could help the team understand the reasons for the instructional strategies and delivery I recommended. Nearly every time I meet with a teacher, she can give an accurate list of what the student struggles with. Usually, it's Math Ability—school math.

Think about that, teachers. Holly is being judged on her ability to do what is valued in the school system: procedures, or Math Ability. Think about what that does to Holly's future. Think about how that positions her in society. Think about how that might affect her self-worth.

In elementary school, if students think math is hard, they can't or won't do it. If, from kindergarten or first grade, numbers are a struggle for them, and learning procedural models is a challenge, they may think they can't be good at it. Many times, this leads to faulting if they believe it internally, and causes them to label themselves as stupid.

Thinking like this can impede their learning for a long time, even a lifetime. This is because they do not see math the way their teachers or other students do. They doubt their ability and want *the math class part of the day* to be over as fast as possible. That's why I can't stress enough the need to have these positive and transformational math experiences in classrooms. Math experiences will improve Math Ability, Number Sense, and students' self-worth, especially those in Quadrant III.

I noticed that Holly would look up when I spoke, but only when prompted. She would tuck her hair behind one ear. She straightened her glasses quite often, like a nervous habit. I could tell right away that she wished math class was over so she could get back to her drawing. With more prompting and asking questions, Holly gave only the smallest amount of information. The look on her face was passive. It was almost as if, from kindergarten, she had decided she couldn't do numbers, and wouldn't be bothered. I zeroed in on that and did my best to encourage her.

A student in Holly's class took note of a sweatshirt I was wearing. It said *Sesame Street 50*. This happened in the fall of 2019. She asked if she could create a math question based on the information on my shirt (because this is what I have trained students to do—create math questions). So, of course, I said yes. She created the following question and I presented it to the class to solve:

"Your shirt says Sesame Street and has the number 50, so if Sesame Street has been shown on TV for 50 years, and it is now 2019, what year did it begin?"

2019 - 50	When Holly saw this example, she stacked the numbers: 2019 50 At first, she added the numbers, but other students at her table told her to subtract. She subtracted 0 from 9 to get 9. Then she subtracted 5 from 1 to get 4 (which is incorrect). She finally wrote the answer as 2049.

Since Holly had challenges in Number Sense and Math Ability, I wanted her to think of this problem as counting, and with the conceptual understanding that subtraction is distance (chapter 11).

Another Quadrant III student, Mary, has had a completely different math experience than Holly. Mary knew how to *play school* better than Holly. Mary was high spirited, even during math, and tried things, even though she had low Math Ability and Number Sense. Holly was spunky, too, but only out of math class. Even though Mary had similar math gaps to Holly's, Mary's attitude and ability to work through challenging math was completely different. Why?

It was because of Mary's exposure to math experiences. Mary was part of a select group of students, taught using the Achievement Formula. Mary's teachers from Kindergarten to second grade used this instructional method. Mary was first exposed to these math strategies and was told to her that math time was for making Mathineers. She had positive, gap-filling experiences for three years. I had instructed her teacher in kindergarten, and the teacher encouraged her to use strategies that created learning for her. Unfortunately for Holly, she did not have access to this math experience.

As we took Mary through different math experiences, her ability to do the procedures and to conceptually think through examples increased. Here is Mary's response to the following question.

What do you know about five sixteens?	Mary was in grade 2 at this point and could very easily combine five tens and five sixes by drawing dots in groups.
	Then she would chunk count. She added 50 and 30 to get 80.
Tell me what you know about five sixteens.	Even though Mary is a Quadrant III student, her math experiences in school focused on improving her conceptual understanding of number and she had greater success than Holly, who had typical math instruction each year.
	This computation situation (five sixteens) actually came from a Reference Task that Mary connected to, referred from the previous school year, that ultimately helped her accurately solve the computation, as well as reason through the situation.

Mary's confidence in math had increased to a point that if you asked her about math, she would tell you, "I'm good at it!"

• • •

Take a look at RyAnn, our final example for Quadrant III kiddos. She was a petite girl in 2nd grade. She is soft-spoken, but a thinker, and can play the game called school really well. She was a pleaser and a rule follower who knew she had to just get through things and the rewards would come. She was also a sweet talker, and she knew how to work the teachers and the system to her favor, so she made an effort to mimic well.

When I asked RyAnn to solve for 32 - 6, she gave me the number 34. How? What happened? Let's break that down to see what the challenge was. I could tell right off the bat that RyAnn struggled with procedures. She did not stack the problem correctly. She also does not have a conceptual understanding of subtraction (as distance), but when prompted with how far apart the numbers 6 and 32 were, she was able to work through and get a more reasonable answer, if not completely accurate.

RyAnn had some success solving math equations conceptually, but struggled with counting precisely. She defaulted to counting by ones which was not efficient in most scenarios. We wanted her to "chunk count" which is skip- counting by chunks (10's, 5's, 2's etc…) or counting in chunks to the next 'ten' number. For example, when counting from 6 to 32, we would chunk the count from 6 to 10 (which is 4) and then 10 to 30 (which is 20) and then 30 to 2 (which is 2) for a total count of 4 and 20 and 2 which is 26.

She could independently work through the conceptual prompt without step-by-step help from the teacher. Her conceptual understanding was increased through actively trying things, with the teacher facilitating her experience through questions like, "Tell me about…" When I have students talk and act out math at the same time, they use more active senses, and more learning takes place.

32 - 6	When RyAnn saw this equation, she stacked the numbers, but then proceeded take 6 from 2, and got 4.
	Then she brought down the 3 and wrote the answer as 34.
	She did not understand the steps of the algorithm, or the concept of subtracting ones from tens.

When I asked her a few clarifying questions to understand her thinking, she produced the following:

| 32 – 6
How far apart are 6 and 32? What is the distance from 6 to 32? | I asked:
How far apart are 6 and 32? What is the distance from 6 to 32?

She became much more confident in her ability to answer these questions. She quickly began at 6 on a number line and counted up to 32. She got an incorrect answer of 27, but a better wrong answer than 34. Although she was still inaccurate, the counting strategy would support increasing her Number Sense. She counts by one's, and once she gets comfortable counting in chunks to the nearest ten and on, she will continue to improve her accuracy. |

Can you see where RyAnn's confusion was with the procedure? She was not able to understand the algorithm of stacking the numbers from top to bottom. However, she had some clarity with questions aimed at a conceptual target. She was able to understand the direction her teacher was moving her and found the solution in another way.

Does that mean that all her gaps are filled in? No, but she is making movement from Quadrant III toward Quadrant IV. Think about the three students we have here. Mary doesn't realize how she might struggle with traditional math instruction because she has consistently been guided with the Achievement Formula. She has the same initial math gaps as Holly, but because of this instruction and experience, her attitude, growth, and efficiency have filled in her gaps and given her an advantage.

Holly has never been exposed to this type of math experience. At the time that I was working with her, she was passive and didn't seem to enjoy a challenge. However, the more experiences we did with her, the more her Number

Sense began to improve, and she had progressively less and less confusion with procedure.

Because RyAnn knew the importance of school and making good grades, she was willing to learn, and started in third grade to see improvements and gains as she works through problems with her teacher's guidance.

Quadrant III students will always struggle, but not as severely in the long term, if they are exposed to more positive, targeted math experiences. Students need a combination of instruction: Traditional math instruction which focus on procedures, and *The Achievement Formula* as described in this book. We begin with their strengths and connect them to their gaps. If their strength is procedures, we can start there and connect it to the meaning and conceptual thinking.

The bottom line is that from years of teaching, being an instructional math coach, and conducting more than a decade of research, I have discovered that all kids improve in their understanding of math if teachers take students through a conceptual experience prior to teaching them the step-by-step breakdown of a procedure.

If we make instructional changes at any level, preschool through high school, it won't guarantee filling in all the deficits, but it will close some gaps and move them toward gaining at least one strength, probably improving another, and definitely not having deficits in both areas. That will be an excellent outcome!

8
FALSE-POSITIVE— QUADRANT II

HOW MANY OF you loved to "play school" for one of your imagination games while growing up? Were you the teacher or the clown? Were you the Hermione of the class or were you the shy one who never spoke up? I'm sure some of you had a blackboard easel, little kiddie chairs and possibly a table.

You would gather your siblings, friends, or stuffed animal toys to be pupils and you would launch into the imaginative game of playing school. Playing school admittedly means that all know the rules, both written and unwritten social rules, all will get the right answers, all will want to learn, and the imaginary play will be fun, but no actual learning needs to take place. Any way you played this game, it was simply fun!

Now, as teachers, how many of you see a similar "game" being played out in your classrooms? The game of students knowing the rules, both written and unwritten social rules, getting the right answers, and wanting to learn. In addition, no one makes a mess or mimics what you are doing disrespectfully. Students who play school well are the students who follow the rules, including the social rules of pleasing the group and performing what is asked of them. They will get their work done to please you and get the good grade or the right answer. These students like procedures, and mimic correct behavior well.

They copy what you are doing and keep things rolling. You, as the teacher, may occasionally want to see some breakthroughs happen in the group with a splinter skill, but for the most part, students will mimic what they see up on the whiteboard. They will ask to see an example and attempt to plug in a different set of numbers.

When the numbers and applied procedures don't support concepts, it merely becomes a game of getting the work done, checking off boxes, and getting a grade. The worst part about all of this is that parents, state tests, and legislators praise the procedural part. Students are rewarded for correct responses, not for effort, trying new things, or exploring possibilities.

Here is a review of the four fluencies discussed in Chapter 5:

1. Procedural Fluency
2. Conceptual Fluency
3. Mental Fluency
4. Fact Fluency

All four of these are absolutely essential to maximize student progress.

Figure 8.1

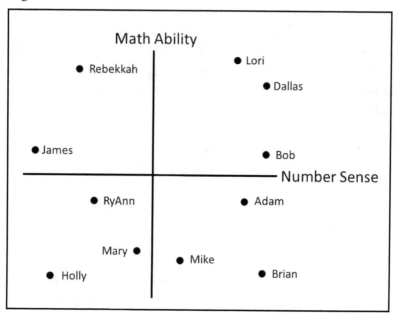

Society values procedural math. If students can't figure out or mimic a procedure, they may be labeled as not good at math. Can you see from the discussion thus far, that Rebekka and James, students who struggle with comprehension, but excel at procedures, may receive similar grades, and be thought to be as good at math as Lori, Dallas, and Bob, who have better comprehension? On the other hand, Adam, Mike and Brian struggle to demonstrate their superior conceptual Number Sense any better than RyAnn, Mary, and Holly, who are deficient in Number Sense, because they don't have proficiency with Math Ability.

This discrepancy in accurately assessing and thus, understanding the needs of students for improved instruction, leads to separation in school and in society that can significantly hinder the progress and growth of students for generations. What do I mean by this? If you have math challenges, suddenly you fall into a separation of class, meaning your opportunity for doing things that have a math base in possible future employment like engineering and many of the sciences, can be slowed from discouraging to nearly impossible.

False-Positive students get all the benefit of having praise in the school for being great at math. But this leads to them a false belief in their abilites Their math success gets shaken at some point in their life. They have been led into thinking that procedural functions are how math is, until they hit calculus, algebra, or a math concept they can't explain. To extend the concept, people in Quadrant III and even some in Quadrant IV never get to be a part of the math-savvy society. They may even face economic challenges for the rest of their lives.

This is why my book, *Making Mathineers*, is crucial to helping teachers know that there are ways to improve not only the four fluencies, but accuracy, flexibility, and efficiency. All have their place in understanding how to increase Number Sense and Math Ability. I hope to help you see how we as a society look at the fluencies, and how we play and accept the game called "school."

● ● ●

As a teacher, I try to extract *thinking* from my students. Thinking looks and sounds like students playing with relationships between numbers. They are willing to explore, talk, and visualize, through models, using reason to solve math. Thinkers are also able to represent math and teach it to others because they understand and can apply it.

> I cannot teach anybody anything, I can only make them think."
>
> — Socrates

However, many students in my first few years of math classes were not adept at thinking.

That was because I was not an expert at teaching them how to think mathematically, and instead, focused on teaching them procedures. Those that mimicked well and were good with facts seemed to be better thinkers, but this was inaccurate. I'll share more about that in Chapter 15.

Do you remember when we met Rebekah in Chapter 4? It was a quick flash of her and her mom going into their apartment. In the classroom Rebekkah was quiet and reserved, socially. She observed lots of things, may have been regarded as a nerd, and was a rule follower. She also knew how to get results in math. First off, Rebekkah's fact fluency was solid.

Rebekkah knew how to skip count by 5's, 10's, hundreds, and thousands from any given number. She understood her multiplication and division facts. Her grasp on telling time and reading an analog clock were spot on. Money facts were easy for her, including understanding the value of money, the names of coins, and how to use skip counting to add nickels, dimes, and quarters. She could tell how many inches are in a foot, the number of feet in a yard, and how many feet are in a mile. She knew how many cups or quarts there are in a gallon.

As a first-year teacher, when kids came into my class that already knew how to efficiently count, knew a ton of measurement facts, and could rip through multiplication facts, I didn't worry about them. They appeared to be great at math, so we got down to procedures and got the work finished. Rebekkah was so good at recalling facts, that as I would teach her procedures, she would plug in and go! Her procedural fluency seemed to match her fact fluency, at least during the year I taught her.

She was so much fun to teach that first year of school because I could simply share the procedure and she would apply her facts and take off! She knew how to play school incredibly well, so I felt that her future was bright. She went through the year without much struggle, in spite of her parents being divorced, having to move, and being labelled "one of those apartment kids."

Now let's go back to Quadrant II, where Rebekkah is plotted. Remember what chapter we are in: False-Positive. What is lacking in Rebekkah's math skills? I have to ask this question, teachers: how many of you have these students in your class, and you have not been worried about them because, for the most part, they look like they are getting it? Are you feeling uncomfortable—a little squeamish? Good. Then you are getting it.

False-positive students know how to play the game of school really well. They can mimic procedures and they have decent fact fluency. This is *Math Ability*. But they don't have a very strong *sense of number*, and in fact, because they can mimic procedures so well, many of these False-Positive kiddos get well into junior high or middle school before their problems are revealed.

Math Example for Rebekkah

What is 20% of 80?	With this as a Target Question and a request that she do it in her head, her quick answer was 4. She divided 80 by 20.
80 x 0.2 0	When asked to do it on paper, she did the procedure she was taught, which is 80 x 0.20. She stacked the numbers and did the algorithm, then realized the answer was not 4, but 16, and she looked confused.
80 x 0.2 16.0	But with a follow up question "How would you solve 20% of 80 by using division?" She did not know. She said she thought she would divide by 20 but that doesn't work. This is a typical misconception at the secondary level for students who lack Number Sense. This quick assessment of Rebekkah justifies the Quadrant II placement and uncovers that the next best instructional step is to improve her conceptual understanding.

James is our other kiddo in Quadrant II, and the name of a female student, so don't let the traditional boy's name of James throw you off. She was a student who truly could be outspoken. She was confident in her questions and meticulously honest and aware in advocating for herself and others. James was an interesting student. She attended private school to get extra help in her academics. She had an education plan, but because she was in a private school it was technically not an IEP (Individual Education Plan), but what we call an Education Plan. This means that a team looked at her needs and set up a plan to help her with the academic gaps in her education.

James needed intervention in several subjects, but we will stick to the topic of math for now. She knew how to play the game of school because she was a rule follower, a social pleaser, and a performer. What threw off the teachers was James' ability to *do math,* meaning she could follow an example set in front of her in such a way that it was tricky to detect any lack in understanding. James could mimic procedures and get answers. Teachers would report that on some units she understood things and followed along, while on other units, she had no fact fluency, mental math, or conceptual math.

James was a student that, when asked the target question, "What time is a quarter after 3?" says 3:25, which is the best wrong answer. She also gave the best wrong answer of "Divide by 20," when asked the target question, "When finding 20% of a number, what can you divide the number by?" She also doesn't know how many nickels make a dollar, which is a target question that predicts the response to the 20% question.

To better understand James, here is an example to explain her thinking while in grade 7.

Change 5 ¼ to an improper fraction	She can easily follow steps and procedures For example: Change 5 ¼ to an improper fraction. She knew to multiply 4 x 5 then add 1 to get 21 and then write the fraction 21/4.
	When I changed the question and asked, "How many fourths are 5 ¼?" she had no concept. I asked, "How many fourths make 1?" She thought about money, that four quarters make one dollar. With her understanding of money, she had a huge aha—that 4 fourths make 1.
	I asked again "How many fourths make 5 ¼?" but she could not make the jump to the connection using her own pattern.
	I took her through the conceptual process, this time using paper strips and folding. We folded one paper strip into fourths, making explicit that we can do this by folding in half 2 times.
	We then got a second paper strip and did this same process to get 4 parts.
	I asked, "How many fourths make 2?" She responded, "I'm not sure. I need to work through this."
	Together we got another paper strip and she was able to continue talking through the pattern without additional paper strips. I had her use the paper strips anyway, to confirm her reasoning. She said that there are 20 fourths in 5 paper strips, so 20 fourths make 5 wholes.
	Then I asked again, "How many fourths make 5 ¼?" This was still a bit tricky, but she eventually got to 21 fourths.
	Whew! That's a lot but these are the rich experiences that build conceptual knowledge and Number Sense and make math stick (forever learning).

Here is that False-Positive again. On the surface, students seem to be able to complete the procedural math fluency but might struggle in conceptual or fact fluency. As long as they get the right answer, we might call it a fluke and be grateful that they are passing, right? How many of you have had parents who say, "Just teach them (meaning my kiddo) exactly what to do and they will do it." Parents are advocating for getting their kiddo to pass the class so that he or she can get the credit and not have to worry about math class again!

If we are to truly improve Number Sense, we need to look at what is happening conceptually. The False-Positive students in Quadrant II are those who are mimicking well and might know some facts, but if pressed conceptually, they don't know *why* they do the math that way. "That's how I was taught in school." Hence, the game called *school,* or school math.

> We can't improve Number Sense by teaching only procedures. It only occurs through experience.
>
> —Jonily Zupancic

I feel I must also address the problem of *special education* here. What special education means for many teachers and parents is *explicit instruction*: to teach children facts and procedures. Here is the clarification. The strategies, which we will talk about in Chapter 11, are built to help children explore, have conversations, visualize, represent, and formulate expectations. Students that are in specialized instruction need these experiences even more than other children, to make connections first, prior to learning procedures, to equip them to reason and find answers with abilities they have.

This means that students need to *experience* numbers. If Special Education teachers only use explicit instructions in procedures and algorithms, it becomes a barrier to improving Number Sense. All these teachers have done is taught students how to mimic, without any meaning behind it. The students won't know why they need to follow a procedure, or how it connects to numbers and relationships, merely that they can do it. If students of all abilities are exposed to rich mathematical experiences, then following the experience with explicit instructions on how to do procedures can be great practice.

To wrap it all up, False-Positive students are tricky to monitor. Don't get fooled into thinking that because they are great at facts, can mimic, and get good test scores, they have great Number Sense. The target questions in Chapter 10 will help identify our False-Positive group of students.

Remember, they have great Math Ability (or school math) but the goal is to help students move in the coordinate plane towards Quadrant I, by gaining as much Number Sense, along with Math Ability, as possible. All right—ready to find some solutions to all of this unfinished and unopened business? I bet you are ready. I am! I've been waiting for eight chapters to get to it!

STRATEGIES

IT'S A CHICKEN AND EGG THING.

9
PLAY, SAY, SEE, SHOW, KNOW

BEFORE WE DIVE deep into the play, say, see, show, know, I want to ask the vital question, what is a Mathineer? After all, it is the title of the book. It is what I call a math student. It is the word I developed, which takes conceptual thinking as well as Math Ability to become a Mathineer.

A Mathineer is a person who thinks through math, finds relationships, taps into Number Sense, swims in the process of exploring, creating and discovering, and connects concepts to their math abilities. Instructional delivery and math experiences provided by the teacher, driven by prompts and questions to promote thinking and reasoning, have an exponential effect on moving students to Quadrant I and enhancing their position as a Mathineer.

Teachers, it is our duty to deliver high quality math instruction. However, in that instruction we need to take into consideration the students' perspectives. We need to know their experiences and how they think about math they are exposed to. They have more to offer than *school math* can tell us. Many students simply lack the *math language* to share it with us.

As we give assessments and pretests to see what kids know, please understand that nearly all of those assessments are limited. They are not assessing things we don't teach. They are mostly focused, again, on the *school math*. Assessment through conversation is the best way to extract and uncover student perspectives.

Every student has their own mathematical story within them. We are trying to find this story through Target Questions and math experiences. Traditionally, math is usually approached by trying to move students to our way of thinking. "Here are some numbers, make sure to stack them, plug them into the algorithm, etc. Stop! Stop! Teachers, we don't even *know what their thinking* involves. Don't you want to truly discover it?

For example, teachers typically teach math with a sorely limited scope because we focus so much on simply doing procedures, but there is a bigger mathematical story. We are limiting the thinking of students and not expanding it by only focusing on procedures. Students, I believe, have a larger scope and reliability of mathematics than we realize. But we try to squeeze them into a limited version of possibility with what we've experienced and learned as typical math instruction.

The radical part of this book is that it feels counterintuitive. It is a mathematical story. Math in textbooks is grossly disjointed. There is no flow from beginning, to middle, and end if we are only instructing by units or by *school math*. When that happens, it's like we are presenting small pieces of math like a check-off list. It's jumbled and tough for kids to connect to it because they can't follow it.

There are pieces missing from the math story because we value the need to get through it and get it done. Math textbooks are not written like a story or a movie. Math, in textbooks, is presented in a way that might seem linear, but it is actually disjointed because of the need to make sure standards are met and procedures are learned.

When you sit down to watch a movie, there is a progression, a story, and a connection. Let's say you pop in a DVD, but instead of watching the movie from beginning to end you decide to go to screen selection. You start watching scene seven, then scene one, then scene nine from a different movie. Can you understand the order? Are you left guessing and trying to fill in the plot lines, the dialogue, and what the characters are going to do next? Of course, you are. It's not enjoyable and it's super confusing! However, that is absolutely how we teach math.

I want to pull you into this conversation a little more. (I know it's Chapter 9 and all, but we really need to figure this out).

What comes to your mind when you hear these words: *play, say, see, show, know*? Do you think of math? Well, let's start to think about it. These simple words are the foundation of how to have students experience math. Warning! All my middle school and high school teachers, I want you to know that this chapter is for you too. Don't skim or skip but play here with us. Let's rock your world!

PLAY

Think about play. Play is exploration.

What does play look like for you during math? Traditional math looks a lot like this formula:

> "Play is the work of the child"
>
> —Maria Montessori.

1. Teacher talks, asking questions that prompt students to solve.

2. Students listen and answer questions.
3. Questions vary from simple to complex, and time may run out with the complex scenarios.

Hum. Did you have fun with that? Were you playing? Are you satisfied and wish that was how you played during math? No way, right? There was no exploration, no discovery, no question building and no creation from the student, merely the teacher talking, and the student trying to copy and hopefully get through it. My Quadrant III students are dying from the pain!

Ok. Let's start again. Play! We need to have students play with math by exposing them to the concept that mathematics can be explored. Play in mathematics looks like this:

1. Students ask and create questions.
2. Students make sense as much as they solve.
3. Teachers begin with the most complex scenarios and leave them unfinished.

Wait! Did you say leaving work that was unfinished? I know I can hear a few of my Quadrant II teachers freak out a little bit. But what about the answers? Students need to give answers and solve problems. This is math after all. There is an answer somewhere. Leaving things unresolved is tough for some, but it is not impossible.

Let's keep pushing on this. Teachers test yourselves. Can you leave the problem unsolved just to play? I think you can. We are exploring and exposing math to kids in a way that builds conceptual thinking and creativity. Here are some great ways to play. You can think of it as exploration if that helps to settle your mind.

Play and exploration needs to be minds-on. How do you turn a mind on? By asking questions. Once minds are on, we need hands on! Touch, flip, move blocks, build, fold paper, and so forth. This hands-on play helps students comprehend and internalize their experiences.

> Play/Exploration:
>
> - Minds-on
> - Hands-on
> - Using math tools like graph paper, blocks, and paper strips
> - Making sense rather than solving
> - Students are active participants.

Minds-on means we are going to give students a stimulus. This is a math prompt without a question that leads students to solving. The purpose of a stimulus is to make sense, not solve. We want students to ask questions and look at the challenge with minds actively working, not to race to an answer. Teachers want to see students think and figure out how to get to the answer.

Hands-on means engaging the physical world with conceptual thinking to increase the ability to recall information. We want the students to be chunking, grouping, moving, and finding connections.

Using math tools to empower the hands-on experience is powerful. For many of us, paper is something we have in the class and can use in many different ways. For example, when we are folding, we may suddenly find we are engaging in counting and discovering. It is a cheap and powerful way to experience math.

Making sense of why thinking, counting, and chunking is happening helps students explore ideas, see other points of view, and stretch beyond a procedure. The focus is not on the answer. The focus is on how this works. Why? Is there a different way of looking at all of this?

The result of having our minds and hands on with the use of the different math tools encourages us to try to make sense of the math experience. Thus, we are active in our math learning and not barely enduring it or trying to get out of it. Engagement makes all the difference in moving toward a different Quadrant. It takes action and work to get there.

• • •

SAY

Let's expand to the next step with *say*. There is a great language component to *say*. In traditional math instruction, who is saying anything and nearly everything? Yes. It is you, the teacher. The teacher is talking and asking questions, prompting students to solve. Remember that we are not always looking for answers.

What are the students doing in a traditional math setting? Students are listening and answering questions, moving from simple to complex. Wait. Having students answer, answer, answer is not the same as having them *say*. Students who are answering are not necessarily expressing their thoughts. We need to facilitate more of what students have to *say*, and shut our saying off, or at least turn it down.

When students are prompted to turn to a partner and discuss a concept (turn and talk) they are highly engaged in the activity. Teachers, this is a gift to all of you. Why? Because you get to hear their thinking. It puts their perspective and needs right out there. As you are hearing how they think, you have the opportunity to see what students know. Then you both can engage in the thinking and saying, learning and teaching together. Teacher and student perspectives can collide to open a new world of mathematical understanding.

When it comes to *say* there are three main components:

1. Students make sense as much as they solve.
2. Students ask and create the questions.
3. Teachers ask thinking questions and give prompts that begin with the most complex and leave problems unfinished.

• • •

SEE

Students need to *see* or be able to visualize the concepts. Teachers, how do you help facilitate visuals? These are the models and structures that we use all the time, like graphing data, placing numbers on a line, using the 120 chart, drawing out a word problem, making rectangles, and folding paper. And when we use rectangles and paper folding, we are also implementing hands-on play. Love that two-for-one bonus.

Ok, so what does *see* do?

Visual models and representations also facilitate higher-level thinking. This exposure is great to support future math learning. It helps to enable communication (*see* supports *say*). Visuals are a powerful way for students to understand abstract math. The representation of the visual with the notation connects conceptual and procedural math.

As a bonus, students can demonstrate their creativity. As students are engaging in this type of math experience, they are connecting the right and left sides of their brain, they are engaged in their work, and they are building synapses—much stronger than anything we could do if we only wanted to see the answer.

In Quadrants II, III, and IV the benefits of visualization and representation, according to Zhang, Ding, Stegall, and Mo are important skills because higher-level math and science courses increasingly draw on visualizations, internal, external, and spatial reasoning to solve problems.

Internal visualization involves "the creation or the recall of visual imagery to represent the information." (Zhang 2012). When I call on students to see, I want them to visualize the problem by creating a mental picture. Students can walk through the process of creating a mental image based on a prompt from their teacher. They can draw images of what they are thinking and seeing in their head to make it more explicit as well.

According to Montague and van Garderen,

"The distinction between internal and external visual representations, many researchers have also outlined differences in visual imagery based on the purpose. Pictorial imagery is used for representing the visual appearance of objects or information. Schematic imagery is used for representing the spatial relationships between objects or information. While both can be used to help students learn and solve problems in mathematics, schematic imagery is more effective as a method for supporting problem solving. Students with LDs[learning disabilities] are more likely to use pictorial imagery when solving problems in math." (van Garderen 2003)

Across the Quadrants the concept of *see* is a powerful one.

● ● ●

SHOW

Now, on the with the show! There are many strategies that help us *show*. As students show, they will use diagrams, number lines, graphs, arrangements of concrete objects or manipulatives, and physical models. We talked about the variety of what these models can look like. In order to have students become successful they will need to learn how to show and use visual models. The models provide students with a way of showing and explaining information. Students will *show* their thinking with these representations.

What about the procedural *show*? Yes, finally! Procedures are important. Now that we have tools to discover the thinking of our students, we can use things like mathematical expressions, formulas, equations, and algorithms. We can even use depictions on the screen of computations or calculations and explain how they represent, stand for, or embody mathematical ideas of relationships.

According to a researcher, C. Anderson, "Such a production is sometimes called an inscription, when the intent is to focus on the particular instance without referring, even tacitly, to an interpretation. To call something a representation thus includes reference to some meaning or signification it is taken to have" (Florian Cajoi 2019).

Wikipedia shares the definition like this, "There are basic, geometry, algebraic, linear algebraic, probability and statistic symbols, combinatorics symbols, Set Theory symbols, logic symbols, calculus, analysis symbols, and, of course, all the number symbols could go on and on. (Florian Cajoi 2019). You grasped the point, I think.

Show is also representing the same thing in multiple ways. This draws misconceptions and reverses errors because students begin to see the many representations of one number or value in dozens of ways. This is a powerful skill for students to master.

We are able to connect the visuals with meanings and use procedural understanding to help explain the thinking that occurs. We must have flexibility within the thinking and construction of mathematics so that math experience can happen for students.

• • •

And finally, we have come to *know*. Here is where we set the expectations. My expectations are simple. All can improve Number Sense and Math Ability. So, since I expect it and I teach my teachers to expect it, the students reach it—and beyond.

The essentials are things like single digit addition and multiplication—at least to think about the distance between the numbers and counting. There are a few need-to-know measurements as well. You'll want to know:

- Addition from 1 + 1 to 9 + 9
- Multiplication from 1 × 1 to 9 × 9
- Inches, feet, yards, cups, pints, gallons
- Skip counting

Know allows for students to share things without getting bogged down. It helps them to increase their confidence, and they become more willing to participate. Little RyAnn is a great example that if she has these "just know" facts down, she is more willing to try and to not quit before she even gets started. You have to love these students.

• • •

With all of this ***play, say, see, show, know***, a student's chance of mastering math has increased significantly; however, there is no guarantee. Improving Number Sense at the secondary level is not intervention. It is part of our regular instruction.

Now for a statistic: in the Johns Hopkins study (also cited in Chapter 1) they looked at Approximate Number System or ANS. This is the cognitive system that gives rise to our basic numerical intuition. According to the study, Number Sense, whether there is a relationship between the ANS and more formal mathematical abilities beyond the school-age years or not, can still increase long after formal mathematical abilities have been acquired.

A second ANS, research study was conducted by the Proceedings of the National Academy of Sciences or PNAS. This ANS dots test (which is an eight-minute, timed test), flashed yellow and blue dots briefly onto a screen, and the participant reported whether there were more blue or more yellow dots. Gathering the evidence needed was conducted in this simple yet clean way. The study reported that, "gradually [math] is refined during the school-age years, with optimal precision attained surprisingly late in life at 30 years of age." (Justin Halberda 2012).

I have a theory that since much of the focus of school is on procedural math, we are delaying the ability to tap into building more Number Sense and cognitive ability. The article goes on to say that, "Success in school mathematics, and our performance in mathematics throughout our adult lives, emerges from many factors. The present findings suggest that one such cognitive component is the precision of the ANS, but this in no way implies that a person's precision is immutable or is determined from birth." (Justin Halberda 2012).

The study continues by saying, "Indeed, the encouragingly protracted course of developmental change in ANS precision and the large individual differences across the lifespan raise the possibility of interventions to improve Number Sense across a range of ages." (Justin Halberda 2012). Again, just to emphasize, our Number Sense doesn't peak until 30 years of age. Wow! That is a lot of time to keep developing and improving it!

I believe that we (schools) are delaying the peak of Number Sense because of the lack of strong instructional practices.

The way we instruct in school decreases students' Number Sense. I believe that these results are enhanced by experience.

Students have to leave school and begin to experience math in real life settings in order to improve their Number Sense and Math Ability exponentially, but many don't even realize their growth.

I discovered through the research that I must expose students to exploration, conversation, visualization, and representation, in order to set expectations for them as soon as possible. There is hope that even though we might begin using this approach late with some students, they will still be able to improve their Number Sense and carry important math concepts into their post-secondary life situations, whether or not that includes further formal math education, such as college, or not.

10
TARGET QUESTIONS—

THEY MARK THE Spot!

What benefit do questions provide? Skip Prichard says, "I never learned anything by talking, only by asking questions." Here are the juicy tidbits you have been waiting for. We are going to focus on eight questions (or prompts) and the concepts they cover. Lest you fear that this might not apply to you, it does—from preschool to high school. Think about the question and how you can ask a variation of it relative to the grade level you teach. Remember my focus is on getting students to think! Students will sometimes say to me, "Will, we ever use this?" I reply with a little sarcasm, "Thinking? Probably not."

These questions and prompts are intended to assess the level of conceptual understanding. They assist teachers in placing students in the appropriate Quadrant in order to determine the best instructional steps for each set of students. I am sharing these with an expanded version of each question, along with the "best wrong answer" to see how the responses for students go. Best wrong answers are the answers that are typically given by students answering incorrectly. There are many other incorrect responses that are less popular. Here some Targets and typical incorrect responses:

Target Questions /Challenges	Best Wrong Answers
1. Skip count by tens from 60 (60, 70, 80, 90, 100, 110, 120, 130)	Best wrong answer is 100, 101, 102, 103, 104.
2. Skip count by tens from 24 (24, 34, 44, 54, 64)	Best wrong answer is 24, 30, 34, 40, 44, 50, 54, 60. Another best wrong answer is 30, 40, 50, 60, 70.
3. Count backward by tens from 62 (62, 52, 42, 32, 22, 12, 2) If students stop here and I prompt to keep going (-8, -18, -28)	Best wrong answer is -2, -12. Another best wrong answer is 0.
4. What time is a quarter after 3? (3:15)	Best wrong answer is 3:25.
5. How many nickels make a dollar? (20)	There are a variety of incorrect answers. The point here is that students lacking Number Sense will not 'just know' the answer 20. They will either have to take time to figure it out, or they will pass on answering.
6. What is the decimal equivalent to 1/8? (0.125)	Best wrong answers are 0.8, 0.08, 0.18, 1.8.
7. What is 20% of 80 (16)	Best wrong answer is 4.
8. What is the value of 2^{-3}? (1/8 or 0.125)	Best wrong answers are -8 and -6.

Simple questions, right? Stay with me, preschool and high school teachers. What do you think you could ask to expand or simplify the concepts? I will give you a few clues to make sure that students are understanding the conceptual parts. Remember, these questions help you target the level of understanding, what the student is missing, and in which Quadrant he or she is placed. Our focus is thinking!

Question: How can we count by tens from 60?
Answer: 60, 70, 80, 90, 100, 110, 120, 130. Here are the best wrong answers for that question 60, 70, 80, 90, 100, 101, 102, 103, 104. Preschool and toddlers can do rote counting by 10s 10, 20, 30, 40, 50, 60.

See patterns with multiples of ten with zero in the ones place? We can also relate this to divisibility by 10 and other numbers that are similar to 10, like 2 and 5, and those that are different from 10 but with their own unique characteristics, like 4, 8, 3, 6, and 9.

Question: How would you skip count by tens from 24?
Answer: 24, 34, 44, 54, 64. The *best wrong answers* are 24, 30, 34, 40, 44, 50, 54, 60. This type of thinking is actually good even though it's not completely accurate! There are many other variations of incorrect answers that are not as good because they lack any type of mathematical pattern.

Why is this important? Assessing whether students understand place value and the base 10 system can facilitate teaching concepts to develop success with conceptual and procedural math by seeing the patterns when counting by tens. Ten is an important number, for base 10 system, rounding algebraic reasoning, and patterns. Efficient counting and operation (like adding and subtracting) are also important for rate and function. Starting at 24 and counting by 10 is like y-intercept of 24 and rate of change (slope) of 10 for a linear function.

• • •

Question: Can you count backward by tens from 62? Correct responses are, of course, 62, 52, 42 and so on, to 2. Students may stop here, so I will prompt them to keep going -8, -18, -28. The *best wrong answers* upon arriving at 2 is 0 or -2 or -12. Can you see why these are? What is the student missing with this concept?

With preschoolers we can assess high ability students! Sometimes we don't ask the question because we think students can't answer. But we *should* be asking lots of questions we think they can't answer. This keeps them thinking, and sometimes they surprise us with their knowledge. At the very least, this prompt will leave a seed of curiosity on which they can build as they grow.

This is a great prompt at the secondary level. Teachers use these target questions for students who still struggle, and maybe always will struggle, with integers.

The first time the skill of operating with integers is introduced is typically in grade 7. This is a reminder that we cannot introduce a concept or skill in the same year we expect mastery. Students who struggle with mathematics achievement will not have enough interactions in one school year to master a concept. We need to expect mastery two or three school years later or begin the conceptual development earlier than the grade level that has the actual standard. And in addition to this, continue the work with these standards after the grade levels specified in the standards.

It's important to note though, that it is not necessary, possible, or appropriate to do this with all standards, because not all standards should be created equal. There are 8 essential math concepts that I define for preschool through high school:

- Efficient Counting
- Number as Shape
- Squares
- Graphing
- Equations
- Fractions
- Factors
- Function

Each of these 8 essentials have a place at each grade level and look different at each grade level. Some of the following concepts should be introduced as early as preschool, but definitely a few years before they show up in the standards:

- Perfect squares (square roots)
- Negative numbers (integers)
- Vertical and horizontal number lines
- Solving equations/conceptually finding unknown values in equations
- Rote counting by fractions
- Time
- Money
- Measurement

Question: What time is a quarter after 3?
Answer: 3:15. The *best wrong answer* is 3:25. Many students in Quadrant II will say this. It's interesting to note that Quadrant IV students give this answer less often than Quadrant II students. Typically, Quadrant III students answer something incorrect other than 3:25 because they do not even make the connection of the word *quarter* to 25, $0.25, and so forth. You will be surprised how many trip over this in older grades. See for yourself whether it is a language barrier or something more.

Question: How many nickels make a dollar?
Answer: 20. But this is a concept they need to *just know*. I want to see that their best strategy, counting in chunks, is better than counting one by one. When I ask this during instructional time, we have the students figure it out, using different tools and strategies, facilitated by the teacher.

What I love about this Target Question is that it is a predictor of students who will be able to find 20% of a number correctly by dividing by 5. Students who don't know the answer to how many nickels make a dollar will divide a number by 20 instead of by 5, to find 20%. This connection helps teachers know early on which kiddos are going to struggle with percentages. But there are instructional experiences we can immerse students in to prevent misconceptions with percent(s)!

Question: What is the decimal equivalent to 1/8?
Answer: (0.125) The *best wrong answers* are 0.8, 0.08, 0.18, 1.8

How much is an eighth of a dollar? Build the concept early on with multiple interactions over time. How does the number 8 and the number 100 compare?

Question: What is 20% of 80?
Answer: 16. The *best wrong answer* is 4. For preschoolers we can incorporate paper folding and number charts to express more about 80. How many tens make 80? How many twenties make 80? Begin conversation about coins and how many have an equal value to one dollar.

Question: What is the value of 2^{-3}?
Answer: (1/8 or 0.125) The *best wrong answers* are -8 and -6.

For preschoolers we can incorporate paper folding in half . . . and half again, and half again. What do you notice? Tell me about what is happening. Tell me about the number of parts after each half fold. Notations of numbers: students may know the value of 3, be able to show 3 things, and subitize, as when rolling a die, but may not be able to write the number three. Understand that when you halve, you double the number of sections, but the pieces are smaller than the whole.

Target Questions are vital for preschool to secondary teachers expanding and increasing students' Number Sense. As you have gone through the chapter and have read the potential that Target questions and prompts have to assess the level of conceptual understanding, will you use them? You can see how quickly the questions assist teachers in placing students in the appropriate Quadrants in order to determine the best instructional steps for them. The concept of understanding the *Best Wrong Answer* with an expanded version of each question demonstrates the responses for the students as well. What target questions are you going to start asking your students tomorrow?

11
THE STRATEGY OF MAKING A MATHINEER

HERE IT IS! The chapter you have all been waiting to get your hands on. The place for answers. The place to finally know what is happening and to get it done. We are preparing strategies that are going to make Mathineers. Ready to start?

A stimulus is anything that promotes mathematical thinking. The purpose of a stimulus is for students to analyze and make sense of the situation, and for the teacher to gain a student perspective. It also gives equal math access to all levels of students and creates an opportunity to make sense of math situations before solving. The goal is not to solve the problems but to extract student mathematical understanding or misunderstanding. Making sense opportunities promote thinking, which leads to creating, discovering, inventing, and reasoning—all of which makes a Mathineer and improves Number Sense.

A stimulus could be a word, a situation, a story, a picture, a video, a number, an equation, a math symbol, a chart or graph, a set of data, or a student response. You can find a stimulus in your textbook resource, online, by creating one, or using one of ours. It is also advantageous to use a released test item as a stimulus to give frequent exposures to the way test items are designed.

Think of it like this. "You can lead a horse to water, but you can't make him drink." I can't make students learn, so to follow up with the horse analogy, we need to make the horse thirsty in order to get the horse to drink. How do you do that? The horse is given a salt lick. I use this same analogy on the students. The Stimulus is the *salt lick* for the students. It is what gets students to learn without forcing them. Teachers, we need to figure out the salt lick. It makes students thirsty for learning it.

For example, a daily stimulus taking 4-7 minutes is ideal. A stimulus can be connected to the lesson of the day, but it's better if it is often unrelated and out of context. This allows students to not have any connection so that teachers can accurately assess math understandings and the level of lack of understanding. It's important to understand student math perspective before we impart our own teacher perspective (which is at times limited).

If we begin class each day with solving, we have students who can solve problems, and students who can't, and others all over the place in between. If we begin class each day with making sense, using a stimulus, all students, especially students who typically struggle mathematically, have the same access to the mathematics. All students can think, reason, make sense, create and invent.

The mathematical struggle for most students is in solving, notation, and symbols. Let's give all students a daily mathematical success with a stimulus and improve motivation, mindset and confidence as well.

When implementing and delivering the instruction for a stimulus, give the class one of the examples below and ask:

What do you see? What do you notice? Or Tell me about...

Students can write ideas, talk with a partner or in small groups, or just share with the whole group. Teachers can document what students say or simply listen. Teachers are not giving their own perspective or instructing on a skill during this time. It is an opportunity for teachers to gather student perspective, assess thinking and make note of the student perspective in order to plan lessons better customized and individualized to student needs. It is better to have students *learn how to think than to learn how teachers think.*

At times teachers can follow up this implementation process with another prompt:

What math questions can you create?

Students create as many questions as they can for the stimulus. It is important that teachers are NOT answering the questions on the same day. Leave the questions unanswered and math problems students create unfinished—salt lick— because as soon as we answer a question and finish a problem, thinking stops.

There are two important steps when preparing and delivering a stimulus to students: 1) Get rid of the noise, and 2) remove the question. Teachers, the noise you want to get rid of is not the noise you hear, but all the extra words and phrases that would lead a student to someone else's thinking and prompt students to solve it.

This instructional technique of getting rid of the noise delivers mathematics in a way that students of all mathematical abilities have equal access to the problem presented during the learning process.

The second key is to remove questions that would prompt students to solve. We will add these questions later in the lesson. Typically, we have students create their own mathematical questions, but not before students have had an opportunity to make sense of the mathematical situation and show their thinking.

When we as teachers and our students are led to retrieve information from our minds, the stimuli prompt ideas to go to long-term memory. Forgetting is necessary for long term learning! So, when we ask students to think about something that may not be what we are currently studying, we want to celebrate forgetting.

The first step in the Achievement Formula is to begin every math lesson with a stimulus – a prompt that allows students to think, not solve.

Here are some examples of different stimuli. Following this list, you will see five subchapters*(11.1, 11.2, 11.3, 11.4, 11.5),* explaining the incredible math I have talked about through the book and more examples. This is some fun free stuff here guys.

Math Stimulus Chart

---

98 and 99

3 and 5

Two boys share 90 candies unequally, so that boy #1 gets 2 pieces for every 3 pieces boy #2 gets.

Joe can paint a room in 3 hours. Sam can paint the same size room in 5 hours.

The area of a rectangle is 24 square inches.

6 → 9
10 → 15
12 → ?

$\frac{1}{3}$ and $\frac{1}{5}$

$\frac{7}{8}$ and $\frac{11}{12}$

$\frac{7}{8}$ and $\frac{?}{12}$

$\frac{7}{3}$

$\frac{4.25}{1000}$

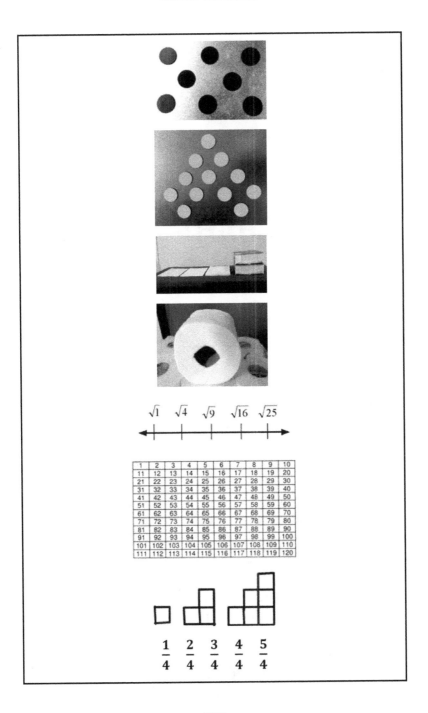

11.1

THE 120 CHART

COUNTING IS A hidden secret of improving Number Sense. It is an underrated and underestimated skill. It is the foundation for understanding the quantity and magnitude of numbers, comparison, and operations. It is a simple task to implement small bursts over time. And it is one of the best ways to become fluent in single-digit multiplication facts. Another way is with making rectangles. We will cover that strategy in a bit.

Counting is essential. It's a vital exercise to engage students in conceptual understanding of numbers. Counting is the basis of rate and function. We underestimate the power of counting as a gap filler for student understanding.

Toddlers count by memory, 2, 4, 6, 8, who do we appreciate. They count by ones, tens, twos, and sometimes fives. They count without understanding value but that is okay and necessary!

If students have not seen a 120 chart before, begin this process with my two favorite questions:

- What do you see?
- What do you notice?

And you can even give the prompt with my favorite three words (besides I love you)

- Tell me about...

Ask the questions proposed above as prompts to trigger *sense making* before going through this exercise.

1	2	3	4	5	6	7	8	9	10
11	12	13	14	15	16	17	18	19	20
21	22	23	24	25	26	27	28	29	30
31	32	33	34	35	36	37	38	39	40
41	42	43	44	45	46	47	48	49	50
51	52	53	54	55	56	57	58	59	60
61	62	63	64	65	66	67	68	69	70
71	72	73	74	75	76	77	78	79	80
81	82	83	84	85	86	87	88	89	90
91	92	93	94	95	96	97	98	99	100
101	102	103	104	105	106	107	108	109	110
111	112	113	114	115	116	117	118	119	120

Here are the questions for the exercises to use with the 120 chart. I have each question separated in a table format so that you can visually understand the process. Teachers, your title will be in bold to help identify prompts for you to say. Please remember that is not meant to be scripted, but to help you understand in a written format some possible conversations to prompt great math experiences.

Question 1

Teachers: Ask students what numbers they could skip count by on the 120 chart to land on 100. Even students in kindergarten have a good understanding of some of these numbers. This is also a great question for high school students to easily choose a variety of numbers, like 2, 5, 10, 4, 20, or 50.

Teachers: Now ask students what numbers they could skip count by that will *not* land on 100. Answers might be 7, 6, 3, 11, 9, 35 or 48.

Teachers: It is time to play. Ask students to choose a number that *does not* land on 100 to count by and check their prediction.

What is the benefit? When students make predictions and test them, dopamine is released in the brain. They can become addicted to math exercises! A good addiction. Students can share what they find out about their number when they skip count. Then they can shade in or circle the number on the 120 chart.

Question 2

Teachers: As a class, we will skip count by 8. (Not 2 or 4 or something else trivial. I like to begin with a tricky number (but not too tricky) so that everyone has a challenge).

What will I find with this exercise? Once we do 8 as a class, I can differentiate for students who struggle by having them do 2 and 4, and can extend, for students who don't struggle, to do 12, which is the next best number after 8. Then other numbers can be explored throughout the school year with this same exercise.

This exercise can be done independently by students eventually. And this is an example of one of the Mathematical Practices focusing on **Repeated Reasoning,** especially when counting by numbers that do not land on 100 such as 6, 3 and 7. This exercise can be done often over time, allowing students to get more interactions. This is another research-proven technique of producing long term learning outcomes called **Spaced Practice** from the books *Make It Stick,* and *Powerful Teaching.*

Teachers: Have students predict if, when skip counting by 8, a count will land on 100. Allow them to experiment and see what happens.

Teachers: Skip counting by 8 does not result in landing on 100. Multiples of 8 include 96 and 104.

Teachers: If we were to give an exact number of skip counts by 8 to land on 100, it would be between 12 and 13 counts.

12 skip counts by 8 lands on 96.
13 skip counts by 8 lands on 104.
For this example, 100 is exactly halfway between 96 and 104, so the number of skip counts is 12 ½.

***Don't force this with students and don't give away too soon! Let them think about it. Even if some students say 12 ½, don't confirm their answer. Once we confirm that a student is correct, all thinking stops for everyone.

We can respond by saying "Interesting," or "Okay we have one thought, what do the rest of you think?".

Teachers: Now that we know that it takes 12 ½ skip counts by 8 to land on 100, we can connect this to paper folding, the Bar Model, and decimal equivalents of fractions. (These strategies are coming).

Question 3

> **Teachers:** Whatever number we are skip counting by—here it is 8—we make 8 the denominator of a unit fraction, 1/8. Then we ask students, "How much is an eighth of a dollar?"
>
> This is another Target Question that can be used for assessment here. Have students individually write on a piece of paper, their name, the date to be turned in, and the decimal equivalent for the fraction 1/8. This is appropriate for grade 4 and beyond. Best wrong answers are 0.8, 0.08, 0.18, 1.8.
>
> For students below grade 4 we ask how much is an eighth of a dollar and have them explore with play. We can use paper folding or the Bar Model to create a rectangle with 8 sections. We could use fake coins to distribute money into 8 spots, until all 100 cents are used up, targeting grade 3 since the problem is 100 ÷ 8.
>
> *** This is a great way to incorporate understanding of money, which is a deficit many students have. There are appropriate ways to facilitate this at different grade levels to get to the point that an eighth of a dollar is 12 ½ cents, technically. We can't have a ½ cent (since we don't have hay pennies) but pretend for the sake of the concept. If students struggle, we can say we have 100 cookies and 8 bags to split them up equally, or 12 ½ cookies in each bag.

> The point is that it takes 12 ½ skip counts by 8 (on the 120 chart) to land on 100, and an eighth of a dollar is 12 ½ cents—the same. Coincidence? Don't answer this for students, but for you, no it's not a coincidence. This works for any whole number between 1 and 100. Try it. Go through the same process:
>
> Pick a whole number to skip count by.
> Figure out the exact number of skip counts with only part of a count landing on 100.
> Make the number you skip counted the denominator of a unit fraction.
> Ask how much of a dollar that unit fraction is worth.

Question 4

Teachers: As an extension for grade levels studying fractions and decimal equivalents, we ask how to write 12 ½ cents as a decimal, in dollars.

*** warning*** Teachers may need to lead this discussion a bit more than in the previous steps. But we write the decimal as 0.12 with ½.

Students usually respond with, "You can't put a fraction in a decimal!"

I say, "I just did!"

It is a perfectly good representation of conceptual understanding. Procedurally and with math notation, we write it a different way, but we need to prove this to students through experience.

Teachers: The point of the exercise is to discover that the exact number of skip counts for any whole number to land on 100 turns out to be the exact decimal equivalent for the unit fraction, with the skip counting number as the denominator.

> 12 ½ skip counts by 8 lands on 100
> 1/8 of a dollar is 12 ½ cents
> 1/8 as a decimal is 0.125

Teachers: How do we transition from 0.12 ½ to 0.125?

We have the unit fraction with denominator 2 from the ½, therefore, we go backward to the 120 chart and skip count by the denominator of the unit fraction ½.

When we skip count by 2, on the 120 chart, we land on 100.

How many skip counts? It takes 50 skip counts to count by 2 and land on 100.

How much is ½ of a dollar? ½ of a dollar is 50 cents.

How do we write 50 cents as a decimal in dollars? $0.50 or $0.5. So, the decimal equivalent for ½ includes the same integer in the denominator as the number of skip counts, 0.50. So if we want to replace the ½ in the decimal 0.12½ then we replace it with '5' or '50' so we get 0.1250 or 0.125.

Question 5

Teachers: One more experience for the 120 chart is to develop the concept of rate and function. When skip counting by 8, we could write the algebraic representation of the function based on a table of values. We can also graph the function.

Let x = the number of times the whole number has been skip counted
Let y = the value at that skip count, which is the number on the 120 chart for that count

(0, 0)
(1, 8)
(2, 16)
(3, 24)
(4, 32)
(12, 96)
(13, 104)

Teachers: This is the linear function $y = 8x$ such that there is a y-intercept of 0 and a rate of change, or slope, of 8 or 8/1. The graph would be linear, a diagonal line going upward to the right with a positive increase. It could be discrete if just looking at whole number counts but could be continuous if looking at parts of counts. This is a proportional situation targeting a constant of proportionality. This math is typically grade 7 content.

Teachers: It is important to begin building this concept in kindergarten, but of course, without the graphing and the formality. Simply skip counting by 8 on a 120 chart and seeing that it does not land on 100 is adequate. The next level would be to learn amounts of a dollar, the decimal equivalent of the unit fraction, and finally, rate and function.

Teachers: The point is that this is a timeless exercise that can be done again and again vertically through the grade levels, with a variety of numbers, with the complexity increasing as the student grows. It is also a nicely differentiated task that the whole class can do by focusing on exploring different numbers.

What do you think about the 120 chart? Does thinking about your students and the Quadrants they are in make you excited to get this started? This is why we have 11.1 chapter especially for you. Your students need it, and they can start tomorrow.

11.2

PAPER FOLDING

WE'VE DISCUSSED THAT in primary grades, students count by ones to 100 and to 120. They skip count by tens, fives, twos, and stretch to fours and threes. This is always counting by whole numbers. This counting will merge into understanding quantity, magnitude, and value of whole numbers.

One error in our instruction is that when students begin to learn about types of numbers other than whole numbers, we don't begin with counting. We usually don't have students rote count by fractions, decimals, or negative numbers. As early as kindergarten we should have students count by fractions, but without the fraction notation. In kindergarten, it is enough to count by halves.

1 half
2 halves
3 halves
4 halves
5 halves

Students don't need to understand the value, just rote counting. And counting fractions can simply be counting whole numbers by ones with a label of the unit that expresses its size.

Paper Folding is the strategy that bridges rote counting with understanding the quantity of fractions.

Paper Folding Process

You may want to play along. You will need a paper strip. I prep paper strips using 8 ½ x 11 sheets of paper. I cut strips the long way to make six 11-inch long strips per sheet.

Before giving each student a paper strip, ask them to predict how to strategically fold the paper to make 8 equal parts. Don't confirm or deny their predictions. Merely listen and respond with, "interesting," and "What do you all think?" You can do this as a whole class or have students turn and talk to a partner for two minutes and then share for three minutes or so.

Now give each student a strip of paper. This process does not require a script. These are simply ideas of facilitating the experience for students. Teachers, your title will be in bold to help identify prompts for you to say. Please remember that this is not meant to be scripted, but to help you understand, in a written format, some possible conversations to prompt great math experiences.

Paper Folding Experience Number 1

Ask students to fold their strips in half.
Teachers: Ask students, How many parts? Answer: 2
Teachers: What is the value of each part? Answer: 1 half, or ½

**For kindergarten, stop here and ask a variety of questions about halves.

Teacher: How many paper strips does Amy have? Answer: 1
Teacher: How many halves does Amy have? Answer: 2 halves

Teacher: Let's count by halves. Use your paper strips to help. Students count and answer:
1 half
2 halves
3 halves
4 halves
Teacher: How many halves have we counted? Answer: 4 halves
Teacher: How many paper strips have we used up? Answer: 2 strips

Teachers, continue to ask and have the students count with the pattern you had established

5 halves
6 halves
7 halves
8 halves
Teachers: If there are 25 of us in class and we each have 1 paper strip; how many halves is that all together? Answer: 50

Yes – this is completely appropriate for kindergarten! Our goal is not to get the answer, our goal is to continue to think about this to create an experience of conceptual learning and building Number Sense, not procedure.

Paper Folding: Experience Number 2

Teachers: Fold the first half and then fold in half again (but tell students not to open up)

> **Teachers:** How many parts will there be when we unfold? Answer: 4 (but the Best Wrong Answer (BWA) is 3**** Listen for this misconception and note, but no need to correct.

Have students unfold to see that there are 4 parts

Teachers: What is the value of each part? Answer: one-fourth or ¼

***We can stop here and skip count/rote count by fourths. We can use paper strips as a visual to connect counting to understanding quantity, magnitude and value.

Teachers: How do ½ and ¼ compare?

Teachers: How many fourths make 25? In other words, if there are 25 students in this class and each student has a paper strip folded into fourths, how many fourths will there be? Answer: 100, or twice as many as there are halves

Teachers: Please ask a number of other questions that can remained unanswered!

Paper Folding Experience Number 3

Teachers: have students fold the first half, then the second (repeating what they had done before) and then folding in half a third time – but NOT unfolding yet!

Have students predict the number of parts when unfolded Answer: 8. But a variety of answers at all grade levels, kindergarten through high school are given.

*** (BWA) are 6 and 7 with students also knowing that there will be 8 parts.
- This is a Target Question in the middle of a conceptual experience that determines the level of Number Sense. Students who know there will be 8 parts have an innately stronger conceptual understanding and Number Sense than students who say 6 or 7. Through this experience, conceptual understanding is increased regardless of the initial level of understanding (or lack of).
- Uncovering predictions, correct or incorrect, releases dopamine that can create a mathematical addiction that these experiences provide. And therefore, students begin to crave this type of mathematical teaching and learning.

Teachers: Have students unfold and see that there are 8 parts and ask why. It's important to have students turn and talk to a partner about why there are 8 parts and discuss the relationship between 2, 4, and 8.

Teachers: Have students skip count by eighths.

Additional Paper Folding Questions:

- How many eighths in 25 wholes? [200]
- How do eighths and halves compare?
- How do fourths and eighths compare?
- How many counts will it take to count to 12 if counting by eighths?
- How many counts will it take to count to 12 if counting by fourths?
- How many counts will it take to count to 12 if counting by halves?
- If the paper is folded in half 4 times, how many parts are there once unfolded? HDYK? (How Do You Know?)

This chart can be made to organize the base of 2 situations.

Folds (Iterations)	Parts	Value of one part
0	1	1 whole
1	2	1 half
2	4	1 fourth
3	8	1 eighth
4	?	?

Here are some final Paper Folding thoughts:

1. One way to conceptually understand 2^{-3} is to identify the 2 as doubling parts each time you fold, or iterate in half, and to identify the 3 as the number of folds. The negative sign in the exponent represents division which connects to the question "What is the value of ONE part when folded in half three times?"

2. To conceptualize 2^0 this would mean that you have done zero folds, or iterations – how many parts? Answer: 1 (strip of paper)
   **You can also visualize and conceptualize 2^x with blocks (see picture)

2^1 2^2 2^3

$\left(2^{-3} \text{ is one unit}\right)$

We can also represent 10^{-3} by iterating 10 parts each time (see picture).

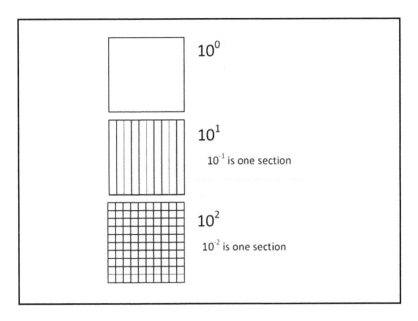

10^0

10^1

10^{-1} is one section

10^2

10^{-2} is one section

Sadly, as this chapter folds to a close, so will we. Ha! Just seeing if you were still with me!

11.3
MAKING RECTANGLES

MAKING RECTANGLES IS another strategy that can be used at all grade levels, with the complexity increasing as we go through the grades. Making Rectangles is a way to develop fact fluency of single-digit multiplication in primary grades. Before facts are introduced and expected to be mastered, they are presented for exposure at those levels. It is also helpful at the secondary grade levels as an intervention for students still struggling to memorize single-digit multiplication facts.

Of course, there are other ways to do this as well, but remember, Quadrant II and IV students may struggle with memorization. We want them to "just know" things too, but memorization may not be the strategy that produces fluency and automaticity for them. Interactions over time with strategies like the 120 Chart, Paper Folding, and Making Rectangles will do this.

Making Rectangles Number 1:

> **Teachers:** Using 24 blocks, make all rectangles possible.
>
> ***Rectangles must be filled in, not hollow.
>
> Build with blocks, draw on graph paper, documenting the height and length of each rectangle.
>
> **Teachers:** How many are possible?
> **Teachers:** Let's count 6 by 4 and 4 by 6 as 2 different rectangles.

From kindergarten through second grade, it is important to begin the conceptual development of factors of a number, without calling these relationships factors. Too often we begin the work of teaching factors in the same grade level that we expect students to master the understanding and fluency of factors (typically in grade 4).

Conceptual development should happen through play and exploration during accessible experiences many years prior to the grade level that mastery is expected. For many students, especially in Quadrant III, more interactions over time are necessary for mastery. Rectangles are the most important shape to explore early and often, with triangles and circles coming in as second and third important shapes. Improvement of Number Sense happens through an exploration of rectangles.

Let's look at examples of using rectangles to conceptualize numbers and procedures through the grades.

Making Rectangles: What they can do for student learning

- Rectangles can be used to build an understanding of even and odd numbers. Given any whole number, use blocks to make a rectangle that is 2 blocks tall. These rectangles are formed by using an even number of blocks. A rectangle 2 blocks tall and 4 blocks long can be made with 8 blocks (8 is an even number). If 7 blocks are used to make a rectangle with 2 blocks tall, you will either need one more block or have one too many blocks. This concept represents an odd number.

- Rectangles can be used to form arrays, and the number of rows and columns are the factors of the number.

- Rectangles can be used to explore the same area using different perimeter problems.

- Rectangles can be used to explore perfect squares and square roots.

- Rectangles can be used to explore multiplication and division.

- A rectangle with an area of 48 square units can have a length and width of 6 by 8 units.

Making Rectangles Number 1

Area = 24 square units

4 units

6 units

Teachers: This is one possibility
Teachers: How many other possibilities?
Teachers: What is the perimeter of a square with area 24 square units?

This is a tricky question because 24 square units cannot make a square with a whole number length and width, but students can begin to explore rational number lengths and widths and they typically say to try 4.5 or 4 ½. This sets up a need to learn how to calculate decimals and fractions.

We can calculate decimals and fractions conceptually with rectangles, and procedurally with algorithms. Now of course I know that the length and width of a square with area 24 square roots is irrational, but students don't need to discover that in grade 3!

With these prompts and experiences, students will have multiple interactions with these conceptual ideas before they get to grade 8, where they begin to formalize irrational numbers. Again, we typically introduce concepts for which we expect mastery in the same grade level, and this sets many students up for failure. It is too difficult to get the number of interactions needed for mastery within a single school year, especially for Quadrant III kids.

Gifted kids need one or two interactions before mastery, bright kids, whose parents think are gifted—ha! need four to six interactions. Our average cognitive ability kiddos may need 10-30 interactions, and sometimes our struggling students or students with learning disabilities may need 60 to 100 interactions!

How do we provide these interactions? By engaging students in experiences based on the strategies in this book, specifically the Making Rectangles strategy, at every grade level during every month of school. The complexity can increase over time, and when it is time to teach procedures, formalize, and give notation to concepts such as irrational numbers, students will be ready for the connection, because of the dozens of conceptual interactions they've experienced over the years.

Making Rectangles Number 2

½ x ½

If this is defined by a 1 by 1 unit square, we can show by drawing a line through it in ½ vertically and ½ horizontally, and the overlap (the upper left section) through multiplication is ¼.

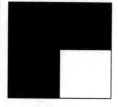

Making Rectangles Expanded:

We can also share that this means ½ group of ½, of which ½ of ½ is ¼. Again, we can show by rectangles:

(4 ½) x (4 ½)

	4 units	½ unit
4 units	16	2
½ unit	2	¼

	4 units	0.5 unit
4 units	16	2
0.5 unit	2	0.25

17 x 38

	30	8
10 units	300	80
7 units	210	56

(x + 2)(x + 3)

	x	2
x	x^2	2x
3	3x	6

Multiplication is area. Teach it connected to making rectangles.

11.4
SUBTRACTION IS DISTANCE

WHEN WE WORK with subtraction, we want students to understand that it is distance we are talking about. Look at all things with subtraction, and you see ultimately that's what it is. We use terms like "take away" and "remove" which are a different perspective, but the phrases, "counting backward" and "counting up" are to find distance and range.

The distance perspective is timeless and transferrable. It keeps its value through the progression of school years, and with new number types. The same sort of thinking can be used as the complexity of numbers grows.

Let's look at this example

Distance Example 1

8-5 means the distance from 5 to 8

Start with the second number (5) and move on the number line to the first number (8)
If you move to the right, positive direction.
If you move to the left, negative direction.
We don't move a negative distance, it's movement in the negative direction, because we're moving toward a smaller number.

Helpful Hint

Watch for students who count 5, 6, 7, 8 and get 4. For example: when playing a board game and moving spaces, students with weak Number Sense will count the space they are on first.

This translates in middle and high school to plotting points on a coordinate plane.

1) Students will struggle to count spaces to plot points accurately if they don't understand distance and how just like on a board game you must move the next square to start counting; you don't count the square you are on to begin with.
2) Students will struggle to set intervals on the x and y axes for this same reason.

Teachers, when you see these mistakes, how do you correct them? Do you allow for exploration and experience to help correct it?
A connecting Target Question is:

> How many hours from 1:00-3:00 p.m.?
> Best Wrong Answer is 3. Correct answer is 2 hours.

Distance Example 2

14-8 means the distance from 8 to 14
These numbers bring another layer of strategy.
Instead of counting by ones, we can move students to chunk counting, getting to 10 and beyond

- Move 8 to 10 - the distance is 2
- Move 10 to 14 - the distance 4
- Put 2 and 4 together and you have 6
- Movement was to the right on a number line because we're moving toward a more positive, or bigger number

Answer is positive 6
**Have this discussion with children in kindergarten.

Distance Example 3

92-48 means the distance from 48 to 92

Chunk count starting at 48

- 48 to 50 (2)
- 50 to 90 (40)
- 90 to 92 (2)

Moving to the right because the number we're moving toward is more positive than where we start

44*Side note: A great way to show these counts is by using a meter stick and count from 48 centimeters to 92 centimeters.

Distance Example 4

92-48 with an alternate chunk counting process
Chunk count starting at 48 might also look like:

- 48, 58, 68, 78, 88
- 48 to 88 (40)
- 88 to 90 (2)
- 90 to 92 (2)

Moving to the right: positive 44

A side note: Some students will stack 92 and 48 without using the traditional algorithm.

2-8 is minus 6
90-40 is 50
50 minus 6 is 44

Stacking without the traditional algorithm:

92
- 48
minus 6 (is 2-8)
50 (90-40)

50 minus 6 is 44

Stacking with the traditional algorithm is procedural and requires regrouping (borrowing). Procedures are necessary to learn, but the process is not conceptual. Remember, there are 2 axes for overall math learning and understanding, the vertical axis (Procedural) and the horizontal axis (Conceptual). Both fluencies are equally important but improving conceptual understanding and Number Sense is the focus of this book.

Distance Example 5

-12-(-7) means the distance from -7 to -12
Start at -7 and move to -12 (this moves to the left because the number
we move to is more negative and smaller than the number we start on).
The direction is negative.
The distance is 5.

So -5 is the answer.
Could also chunk count from -7 to -10 (3) left
-10 to -12 (2) left
(5) left
-5

Distance Example 6

23-(-15) means the distance from -15 to 23
Start at -15 and move to 23 (moving to the right because the number we
move toward is more positive and greater than the number we start on)
-15 to 0 (15) right
0 to 23 (23) right
15 right and 23 right (38)
Positive 38
38

Distant Example 7

-18-12 means the distance from 12 to -18
*Students often ask 'Is that a 12 or -12?'
Be careful answering!
Yes, it can be both with different representation but right now it is written as positive 12
Negative 18 minus positive 12
Yes, a different (equivalent) expression gives the same value
-18 + (-12) and in this expression the 12 is negative

We must be cautious of our language and precision in describing expressions and numbers when clarifying for students. If we oversimplify, we create misunderstandings and misconceptions.

Start at 12 (positive 12)
Move to -18 (left)
12 to 0 (12) to the left
0 to -18 (18) to the left
The distance is 12 left and 18 left (30 total moves left)
And to the left is negative direction
-30

Distance Example 8

-3 ¼ - (-5)
Start at -5 and move to -3 ¼ (right)
-5 to -4 (1 to the right)
-4 to -3 ¼ (3/4 to the right)
1 ¾

**This is very tricky for students! But following procedures is tricky as well and creates a burden to remember many tricks and steps.
It takes many experiences and interactions over time with counting and conversation to master.

Some students may still struggle in high school because they need many more interactions with this idea. Think of how you can devise more experiences for the students to practice this way of thinking.

Math can be complex and if we strip away the complexity to make it easy for students, we may generate misunderstandings and misconceptions that are difficult to reverse. Keep the complexity, focus on the conceptual and give more experiences over time for students to think through, reason and make sense. That is the true way to make a Mathineer.

11.5
DIVISION IS COUNTING

LET'S PUT THIS right out here on the table. When I present, teach, and work with students and teachers about division, I am speaking, showing, playing, seeing, responding, re-teaching, and taking deep dives with them. So, to reach out to you, who feel so far away, yet I know we have gone on an incredible journey together, is tough. I truly want you to get a taste of this and hunger for more.

I never realized the challenge of putting number in a written form until now, but I digress. Here is where we are, so here we go. Bottom line, division is counting but division is visual, therefore it must be experienced by students and teachers as visually as possible. What will we use? That's right paper folding, bar models, and making rectangles.

I bet you are thinking, what is a bar model? A bar model is a rectangle drawn on paper to represent the paper strip from paper folding. The bar model is a visual representation for division, fraction, and other concepts. The bar model is sometimes called a tape diagram. The bar model can be used as a visual representation as a double line and a number line.

We want students to think of division conceptually with the following:

- Sharing equally
- Number of groups
- Number in each group
- "Goes into"
- Skip counting
- Chunk counting

There are many perspectives of division. Using the example $231 \div 7$, we can think through various conceptual frameworks.

We can say that 7 "goes into" 231 a certain number of times. We can answer the question, "How many times do we need to skip count by 7 to land on 231?" Obviously, we do not want to skip count by chunks of 7 to solve this, but when improving Number Sense and conceptual understanding, the goal is not always solving. Skip counting by 7 to 231 is not an efficient way to solve.

The goal is to think and reason about the situation and meaning of division. Division is the number of groups and the number of things in each group; there are 7 things in each group, and I want to figure out how many groups I need to use all 231 things.

This perspective is important when given the division problem $6 \div \frac{1}{2}$ such that we can think $\frac{1}{2}$ "goes into" 6 a certain number of times. We can answer the question, "How many times do we need to skip count $\frac{1}{2}$ by to land on 6?" Since students know how to rote count by $\frac{1}{2}$ through paper folding, they now have a strategy to figure out this division problem without a 'flip and multiply' procedure, which is . . .

How many one halves make 6 paper strips. Students in high school too often give the Best Wrong Answer of 3 for this division problem. With a stronger Number Sense and conceptual understanding, fewer students, if any, would not give the Best Wrong Answer.

Back to the example, 231 ÷ 7, we can chunk count to get to 231. When we chunk count, we count by multiples of a number. Instead of counting by 7, we can count by 70. Let's look at the facilitation strategy for teaching. We will review Mike's (Quadrant IV student from chapter 6) thinking in this chapter with a different example.

What number less than 231 is divisible by 7? 231 ÷ 7	First, ask students
	What is the largest number, less than 231 divisible by 7? (This is actually another great Target Question).
	A typical correct answer but indicating a low sense of number is 14 or 21 or any other multiple of 7 less than 70.
	There are other responses that show a stronger number sense, but 70 is a great response! Still not the best, but I can use this student response to look at multiples of 7 from a different perspective.
	Soon students start to come up with groups, and even patterns 70, 140, 210 Bingo! 210 is great!

| Keep encouraging the students to get to 210. | Some students will give 210 as their first response to the largest number less than 231 divisible by 7.

These are students that have a very strong Number Sense and conceptual understanding (Quadrant I and IV)

The response of 210 is amazing! We can get all students there with experiences over time.
If we are at 210 then 210 ÷ 7 is 30 then we have 21 left and 21 ÷ 7 is 3
So 30 and 3 is 33
Which is 231 ÷ 7

210	21

Instead of counting by 7's to 231, we can efficiently count in chunks, 210 and 21. |

Another perspective of division is knowing how many groups there are and how many items are in each group. Here is the example with the same problem 231 ÷ 7.

| How many in each group?
231 ÷ 7 | The bar model shows 7 groups. Students can use counting to figure out how many in each group. Their level of Number Sense determines how they will count to get started, by ones (one in each of the 7) or by tens (ten in each of the 7).

1	1	1	1	1	1	1

10	10	10	10	10	10	10

This exercise helps teachers assess how strong or weak a student's Number Sense is. Over time we want students to move to more efficient counting and chunk counting (in this case) by tens, or better yet, by 30's.

30	30	30	30	30	30	30

|

We cannot force this type of thinking for students. We must provide experiences over time for their Number Sense to develop. This happens through providing experiences opportunities for students to discuss their thoughts and perspectives with others.

| We have 21 left so we will put another 3 in each of the 7 spots | Once we have 30 in each of the 7 groups, we have used up 210 of the 231. We have 21 left so we will put another 3 in each of the 7 spots.

So, $231 \div 7$ is 33.

Another benefit of this strategy and thinking is that we can answer many other questions with this visual. What is $\frac{1}{7}$ of 231? It is 33. But we can also very quickly figure out from the picture $\frac{2}{7}$ of 231 with 2 of the spots together.

| 30 3 | 30 3 | 30 3 | 30 3 | 30 3 | 30 3 | 30 3 | |

You might be thinking this is not efficient solving. You might be correct. But remember that solving is not the goal. Making sense, connecting to visuals, and improving Number Sense is the goal. This is how it is done.

6 divided by one half.	$6 \div \frac{1}{2}$ Using this same thinking we have $\frac{1}{2}$ of a group. So, 6 is $\frac{1}{2}$ of a group. How much is the whole group? 12 <table><tr><td>6</td><td>6</td></tr></table> There are many perspectives of division. We can think of the related multiplication problem as well. $231 \div 7 = ?$ $7(?) = 231$ $6 \div \frac{1}{2} = ?$ $\frac{1}{2}(?) = 6$

Looking at the examples given here, I recommend looking back at chapter 6 and Mike's example. Look at when Mike started to share, group, and think about what it *goes into*, and skip and chunk counting. I want to emphasize that conceptual perspective of division improves Number Sense. When Number Sense is improved, students will make progress in the Quadrants, and move closer to Quadrant I.

This progression should begin in preschool—conceptually—not procedurally or symbolically. The earlier we begin to engage students in math experiences with division, the more interactions over time they will have with these ideas, and the earlier they will develop a strong understanding of division and Number Sense.

Here is a fact. We don't introduce division until later in the school years because, somehow, we think that there is a progression of operation:

- Addition, then subtraction
- Multiplication

- Division
- Exponents and roots

But the point is, operations are not a progression. Can repeat that? Yes. This is my book and so I will. OPERATIONS ARE NOT A PROGRESSION. We can teach all operations *through* division! Beginning in preschool, if it is conceptually based for any math concept, we should be introducing and engaging students in experiences with division well before the grade levels in which we expect mastery. For many students, conceptual development over time will almost eliminate the need for *math intervention.*

How are you feeling about division as counting? I have so much to share with you about this in my Achievement Formula book. If you want more right away, please contact us. The email, website, and phone information will be at the back of this book. I know you are just getting a taste test of everything here. I have so much more to give and I can't wait to do that for you.

12
CHANGE BEHAVIOR BEFORE BELIEF

"You have to change behaviors before beliefs"
—Jonily Zupancic

HOW MANY OF you have ever sat in a chair at a conference or a workshop and the speaker asked you to get into a group and do something? How many of you, when the request is given, are hesitant even resistant and start to think, "I hate doing things like this." But because of the request and possible peer pressure in the room to comply, you move to the group and begin the activity. As the activity unfolds, you find yourself engaged in the work, you find yourself stimulated, and you think, *ha, that was better than I thought it was going to be.*

What happened in your thinking to make that simple shift? You acted. You did what you were asked to do. You behaved in the experience of the activity; following that and returning to your seat you discovered that your belief was changed.

It turns out that if we engage in a behavior, particularly one we had not expected or wanted to participate in, our thoughts and feelings toward that behavior are likely to change. Doesn't that blow your mind? Take a look at the title of this chapter again, *Change Behavior Before You Change Belief*. Ah, will you look at that. By taking action in something and experiencing it, your beliefs can change.

Warning! Here's the rub. It may not seem intuitive, but if we start to participate in an activity, even if it is a negative one like gossip or even back-talking about others, our thoughts and feelings about that individual will become negative and backbiting as well. Why? You took action in an activity and it changed your mindset. This is a mindset shift that needs to happen. So be careful because it works in both the positive and the negative directions. I saw how negativity impacted a few of my teachers.

Let's take a walk back in time, all the way back to Chapter 3, where we met some of our teachers. Do you remember Liz? She was our fifth-grade teacher and she personally hated math. She feared the cognitive thinking and Number Sense of math based on her math experiences, especially when it came to the number relationship. She knew that teaching math was going to be a struggle for her because of her fear of it. Liz knew she could see a math example and plug things into an equation but struggled so much with her own Number Sense that she could not think beyond that.

Liz stayed in a safe place and she did safe math. She drilled facts, became a worksheet survivor, and her students were able to get through things. There, I did it, done! But math is not meant to be survived or barely gotten through. As a result of her math approach for over 20 years, her students saw no real gains. She and her students were merely surviving.

Liz learned in her school years to survive math, to "get through it" in order to get to the prize on the other side. Why did she think this way? She did not have the foundations to help her understand relationships with numbers.

I have a saying I share with my teachers: "Math is not a hot stove or a busy street. Students will not be harmed trying math experiences." Teachers, you may feel a sense of dread and fear, but this is a mindset. I promise you if you take action and implement the research and the work found in this book, your beliefs will change. Why? Because you took action.

Take Action! Try new things! And the beliefs will follow.

If you don't take action to change a few things, then how will you ever see your beliefs change? Teachers, what are the practices that you are performing right now that are not helping, but you continue to do them out of fear? Do you dare make a list? Do you know what they are? Are you ready to see them, acknowledge them and then make a change?

> "You have to change behaviors before beliefs"
>
> —Jonily Zupancic

How many of you see something at a professional development and think, *I wonder if that will work? I wonder if change can happen.* How many of you start to implement the behaviors, regardless of wanting proof or evidence? That takes a lot of faith and trust, but in the end, what happens? Your actions cause beliefs to change. However, you have to take action first.

Here are a few more of my opinions (Jonily-isms):

"Number Sense can't be taught, but it can be learned and can be improved over time and through experience."

In chapter 7 I said, *"Explicit instruction is the barrier to improving Number Sense."* When we, as teachers, are trapped in fear and overuse explicit instruction (teach to the procedure) instead of conceptual learning, we are not allowing the experience or action to help change our belief.

For students in Quadrant III, trapped in only learning through explicit instruction, is detrimental to their ability to learn. Quadrant III students must *experience* math as well. Let me be clear here. Math experiences are needed in all Quadrants, especially in Quadrant III. Teachers may use explicit instruction when teaching the procedures, especially to students who are in special education. However, if that is all they do, they are limiting their students.

Teachers from special education attend my workshops, learn how to use experience to get math thinking started, and add even more experiences to their repertoire. *"Explicit instruction is for procedures and facts. However, Teachers, you must find out what the students are thinking through the math experiences in order to know what they need."*

I have many teachers who attend my workshops and they indicate they want to have the change happen, but they say, "could you please make it a step-by-step method?" Ah, they are so cute. Here is the crux: step-by-step instruction isn't a good intervention for cognitive thinking; otherwise improving cognitive thinking would require procedural practice.

If there were a step-by-step procedure for improving cognitive thinking, don't you think it would have worked by now? Well like anything else, it takes action, gathering the evidence, examining the data, having mindset change, and challenging beliefs.

When students construct their own understanding through the math experiences, we guide them through, math becomes informal for them.

Let's take a look at this. Teachers, how many of you have these thoughts.

- Jonily has been doing it for 20 years.
- She 'just knows' this.

- How do I replicate this? *Can* I replicate it? What do I do to replicate it?
- We don't like changing our instructional strategies because we ourselves don't know instinctively how to inspire cognitive thinking in our students—like it freaks us out.
- I only know how to do this procedurally. I'm terrified to let the students be free conceptually.
- Students can't get it.
- Students don't have the developmental understanding to do conceptual reasoning.
- I tried. It's hard. I'm more comfortable mimicking procedures and representing them.

There are difficult instructional strategies for both outcomes, but both are important. Some parents, teachers, and administrators don't believe in focusing on conceptual understanding of mathematics and its importance because they, themselves, have poor Number Sense. Teachers who are in Quadrant II will cast a lot of fear on the idea and will want to stick to procedures.

Come on now, let's take action and change our own thinking for the benefit of our kiddos. How can we expect students to think when we, ourselves, fear it? It is going to take some practice, but that is the nature of teaching. It is a craft that can improve with each class, each year, mostly because of the growth of the teacher.

Remember to always use these prompts when developing cognitive thinking:

- What do you see?
- What do you notice?
- Tell me about...
- What math questions can you create?

Warning: Uncovering student perspective extracts some remarkable things that students know, which we can use to advance their knowledge to the next level, but this extraction can also reveal misunderstandings and misconceptions they have carried with them for years. We must make note of these things during this phase, but not try to fix these thoughts or fill the gaps right away. Through experience and with procedures we will know how to guide students toward Quadrant I, filling in the gaps along the way.

"If *I* say it, they hear it. If *they* say it, they learn it."
—Jonily Zupancic

There is a belief of priorities and importance in what we want students to know mathematically. You know it's not up to me in this book to tell you which one is implanted. As a reminder, look at Chapter 11. I have examples of how to extract student perspectives with a stimulus, like a, word, symbol, picture, video, number, equation, pattern, or situation.

The power of this book, *Making Mathineers,* exposes teachers to know how to give instruction in both conceptual thinking and procedural thinking. I know that if you act with all the math that has been shared with you in this book, you will start to believe it. Teachers, your action will change your belief. Some of you may alter your beliefs as you focus on procedures only, to a balance of actually applying conceptual experiences, because you now know how to use them with a stimulus in your classroom. This is wonderful!

Others of you may only want to enjoy a swim in the conceptual and never quite get to the struggle of creating and figuring out how to apply procedures to the student's thoughts, because that's going to be hard. But now you know the need for math ability as well as conceptual ability, and you have skills to help in both areas. Wow! This is great work.

Now, to close out this chapter, I'd like to address the elephant in the room for just a quick second. Teachers, you have learned throughout this book that both conceptual thinking and procedural thinking are needed. I want to be clear that I support both.

Conceptual vs procedural or old math vs new math is not an either/or argument for me. Math is a universal truth. There are rules, supports, answers, and absolutes with math. Math does not have to be polarized into the old vs new math. If you feel you are ever forced to choose sides, please don't. Embrace what math is. It is both.

If districts say, "We are a procedural school," or they say, "We are a conceptual school", they have the moral obligation to tell the parents that. Parents need to be aware of how this can impact the future of their student. Administration and school districts need to inform parents that if procedural math is what they value and spend all of their time, energy, and effort on, or if they have students "swim in conceptual ideas and thinking" without the struggle of creating and figuring out how to apply procedures to their thoughts, students will fall short in both areas.

Remember that I support conceptual math (the experience of math and Number Sense) and the procedures of math (Math Ability or School Math). Both are needed and there are no sides here as far as I am concerned. If we are forced to pick sides, then no one wins. It is not good.

I hope that everything we have discussed in the book thus far has started to entice you to take action, see results, and influence your belief. Following what you have learned here will prepare you to magnificently improve your math instruction for your students.

SUCCESS

WATCHING THE PLOTS ON THE QUADRANT MOVE!

13

LOOK AT MY PLOT, I MOVED A DOT!

HOW DO WE get students to move within the coordinate plane toward Quadrant I and further to the upper right corner of Quadrant I? What needs to happen? Now that we have gone through the strategies and can see *play, say, see, show, and know* power, we have The passion it takes to make a Mathineer.

Starting in Quadrant II our, false-positive students, let's remember that they have a strength in procedural thinking, but are weak conceptually. These students mimic well, so we must increase their conceptual experiences with the use of questions. Teachers, in asking the questions we are able to clearly see their learning, but we are also able to prompt them to increase their conceptual knowledge when we change the questions.

For example, if the question is, "Subtract 278 from 534," these students stack and subtract because that is what they are good at. Let's change the question to, "How far apart are 278 and 534?". (Remember from sub-chapter 11.4 that subtraction is distance). This question is important because it is timeless and transfers to all other types of numbers.

Here's what I mean by timeless and transferring to all types of numbers. If we ask students to subtract 7 and -3 or 534-278 the procedures are different. But when we ask how far apart the numbers are, conceptual thinking for the student is the same. Students will fill in parts to the next whole number and multiples of ten. This process improves conceptual thinking because it highlights the value, quantity, and magnitude of numbers, and therefore improves Number Sense—which is conceptual.

Do you remember James from Chapter 8? She is a student that, when asked the target question, "What time is a quarter after 3?" says, "3:25" which is the Best Wrong Answer. She also gives the best wrong answer, "Divide by 20," when asked the target question, "When finding 20% of a number, what can you divide the number by?" She also doesn't automatically know how many nickels make a dollar, which is a target question that predicts the response to the 20% question. Knowing what you know now, and having some tools to increase her exposure to concepts, by reasoning and experimentation, what would you do to help increase her conceptual knowledge?

Overall, to fully impact and help our Quadrant II students move toward Quadrant I, there are questions we need to ask that will help them increase their conceptual experiences. How we get this group to actually move is to improve their counting. The top three ways to do that are:

1) 120 Chart
2) Paper Folding
3) Making Rectangles

Moving on to students in Quadrant IV, our false-negatives, they are the exact opposites of Quadrant II. Quadrant IV students have strong conceptual thinking. Teachers, we need to provide experiences that will help these students connect their thinking to the appropriate procedures. Students in this Quadrant can also be misunderstood and even labeled as having weak math knowledge. They can score low on tests because they lack confidence in application of procedures.

However, the great news is that moving from Quadrant IV to Quadrant I is only one step. It is increasing procedural skills. With the process "I do, we do, you do" we first must be aware of the conceptual thinking of the student so that we can connect their thinking to the procedure.

Quadrant IV students don't need to master all the achievable procedures if their thinking has been embraced and celebrated. This is enough for them to use their knowledge to perform well. In traditional math instruction, these students are always trying to detect how their teacher solves problems, and searches for the correct procedural approach. If it's not compliant to their way of thinking, they will not perform well, will continue to devalue their own thinking and understanding, and continue to have high anxiety with low confidence.

Students in Quadrant III are special. They are true negatives—weak conceptually and procedurally, but all is not lost. We can still help these students. Moving students from Quadrant III to Quadrant I takes savvy teaching skills. We must first move Quadrant III students to Quadrant IV by increasing conceptual understanding and confidence and decreasing anxiety. Once we have provided experiences that move them closer to Quadrant IV, we can connect those experiences to the symbolic, abstract, procedural approach as we constantly and consistently toggling back and forth from conceptual to procedural instruction and guidance.

For the mathematical lifetime of these students, they will need to go back and forth with these approaches because the conceptual experiences will increase their Number Sense. Success and confidence in the procedural lessons will allow them to see math in *math language* like society wants them to see math. It's through this process and connection that they will move closer to Quadrant I.

If we try to move Quadrant III kids to Quadrant II first by stressing procedures, they will remain stuck in Quadrant III. The procedural approaches continue to stress these students out because they do not see math this way. The only way to get them to understand procedures and symbols is to first get them to understand the value of numbers, improve Number Sense, and then improve procedural skills.

The strategies in this book focus on increasing conceptual understanding (for Quadrant II and III kids) because teachers are typically already good at teaching procedures. It's when we teach procedures and kids don't get it that we need the methods in this book to guide our instruction.

Moving kids to Quadrant I with improved conceptual skills increases their available strategies.

The number 1 secret to improving Number Sense is *counting*. Experiences with counting increase the understanding of Number Sense exponentially. All of these strategies increase and improve Number Sense with counting.

1. 120 Chart
2. Paper Folding
3. Making Rectangles
4. Subtraction is distance
5. Division is counting

Next, is the Big Idea

A Stimulus is an opportunity for students to make sense of a mathematical scenario before doing the work of solving – a way for teachers to gain student perspective. Teachers, use a Stimulus to tap into student thinking and to know which Quadrants students are in.

When we ask students to solve first, we have kids who can and kids who can't, and many others somewhere between. By focusing on solving and starting lessons with solving, we separate students into groups: kids who can and kids who can't solve and all other kids in between. We create a need for differentiation because kids are on different levels.

When we begin lessons with *making sense* by using a Stimulus, we allow access to all ability levels and it naturally differentiates. We want students to make sense daily, before solving. This allows students to articulate their thinking and an opportunity for their thinking to be honored and valued. This increases confidence and decreases anxiety.

Many times, I ask students to create their own mathematical questions as a part of the process of making sense. Here is a list of questions that one student, Bob, created:

- How many two-eighths make 24 wholes?
- How many one-fifths make 24 wholes?
- How many two-fifths make 24 wholes?

Bob came up with that list because he was exposed to mathematical experiences.

When I was structuring this book, I actually had Mary from Quadrant III placed as a Quadrant IV student because she had been using these strategies for over three years and she loves math. She claims she is good at it. She is in a cohort of students and teachers who will continue to use these instructional strategies through the eighth grade with her. From what we can see, she is developing her Number Sense, and is able to break through the barriers that have held her back.

Brian was labeled as a Quadrant III student because the focus had been on his behavioral needs and lack of support in the classroom. But through the use of target questions, we could quickly assess that he was actually a Quadrant IV student. His cognitive abilities demonstrated that he actually knew a lot more than teachers thought. He simply needed more help with the procedures.

The list goes on and on. What I want you to do is to think about your students, ask target questions find out what Quadrants they are in, and then make your plan for math experiences to move them as close as possible to Quadrant I. Teachers, you have all the tools to help plot the students on the Quadrants and move them closer to Quadrant I than ever before. I can't wait to see their progress and yours!

14

HEY TEACHERS, LET'S CHAT!

LET'S TALK ABOUT change and implementation. In Chapter 3 you were introduced to 8 teachers who are teaching in a variety of settings from private to public, rural to urban, and from 3 years to 25 years teaching. I wanted to give you a broad range to see what happens when teachers implement the instructional practices talked about in this book. Teachers take their students on a journey to becoming Mathineers. I wanted to know the changes that had occurred since you (readers) were introduced to them in chapter 3.

The list at a glance:

Name of the teacher	Years teaching	Setting
Jill	25 years	Urban, High School
Jennifer	20 years	Rural, Grade 7
Amy	3 years	Suburban, Title I, Grade 6
Liz	25 years	Suburban, Grade 5
Rachel	20 years	Suburban, Grade 2
Linda	15 years	Suburban, Grade 1
Karen	5 years	Urban, Kindergarten
Donald	15 years	Rural, Grade 4

● ● ●

Jill

"Jill, good morning! Thank you so much for being willing to share your experience here."

"It is my pleasure."

"Fantastic! Let's get right to it. When we first met, you told me that you had many challenging students. And they not only struggled with math but were no longer interested in math. What has changed?

"It's simple really. You showed me one thing that changed my approach to my instructional practice with high school students. You taught me how to get rid of the noise and remove questions."

What happened when you got rid of the noise and removed questions?

"It forced students to find reasoning and sense-making. When the noise was removed and I was not pecking away at them, the students actually gave me their perspective. I could see right where they were, and how to move them through the different Quadrants."

"What is the most noticeable difference in your classroom?"

"Students loved this from the first time I implemented it. It was game-changing, fresh, new, deep in thinking, and all of the students could be involved. In fact, the biggest difference was that they were the most engaged of any students I had taught over the past twenty-five years."

"What has changed for you?"

"I stopped marking down the days in my teacher retirement calendar. I now look forward to teaching and engaging with the students. I don't want that to end because I know that I am making a difference with the students; whereas, prior to clearing the noise and removing the questions, I wasn't. Now, I know that I am."

● ● ●

Jennifer

"Jennifer, how has the day been treating you?"

"Great. No complaints."

"Wonderful. When I contacted you a few weeks ago and asked you if I could interview you for this book, you had one of the best responses of all my teacher candidates. Do you remember what you said?"

"Yes! I said that if my words can save another math teacher from quitting, then I'm all in!"

"What stopped you from quitting?"

"I needed to have something that was not a fad, not part of the "latest and greatest" research, only to be replaced again by another person's idea every 3 to 4 years. I have been teaching for over 15 years in rural middle school and I have seen about 4 different math trends during that time."

"What were some of the trends?"

"It all had to do with the math war, *Old math vs New math,* and all the ups and downs and debates with it. Depending on which school and the administrator, we would teach 'old math' or it would switch back to 'new math.'"

"What changed for you?"

"When I attended the two-day workshop, I discovered that you were not there to pick sides. You were there to show us that conceptual and procedural math thinking are both needed. That was so refreshing. I was hooked!"

"Thank you for those kind words. As I'm sure the readers of this book will experience that for themselves, can you share with me what impacted you the most from the instructional strategies?"

"Yes. It was the daily stimulus of prompting with, 'What do you see? What do you notice? and, 'Tell me about it.' Those simple prompts transformed student engagement and had me wanting to go and teach other teachers about the process. I started sharing the implementation of new approaches with anyone who would listen."

"That is so exciting to hear. Was there anything else that you shared with your fellow teachers?"

"Absolutely! The other secret was the textbook. I told them to use a textbook as a resource. It's just a resource! The book does not dictate the instructional design and delivery process. The textbook now enhances my instruction rather than hinders it. And my fellow math teachers at the middle school now use it in the same way. So, we have four teachers making big impacts on over 400 students! This is the game-changer."

● ● ●

Amy

"Good Morning, Amy! Thank you so much for agreeing to this interview!"

"You bet! I just had to share the excitement to help another teacher out there that is struggling the way that I was."

"Super cool! Thank you. Can you tell me what happened during one of the exercises that we did? Because I know I will never forget your face."

"Oh my gosh! Yes. You are talking about the time you made me cry during professional development. You had given us a target question, 'What is the value of 2^{-3}?' I found myself scrambling to explain fractions and decimals. I was pretty much freaking out. It was that moment of, *wait a minute! I really don't know math!*"

"I remember looking at so many other math teachers and they were just scribbling down answers and I was like, *I'm out! Without a visual or a resource like a textbook I don't know what I'm doing!* It was that moment when I figured out that I was a Quadrant II student! It was like 15 years of schooling had been stripped away in a few questions. So yes, a lot of tears that day."

"But what happened to make the difference for you? What stopped the tears?"

"What stopped the tears was Rebekkah's story. I figured that you were a Quadrant II student just like me and yet you didn't quit! You figured out a way to build and improve your Number Sense. You improved your cognitive thinking! I thought, if she could do it, then so could I!"

● ● ●

Liz

"Afternoon Liz. We have known each other for a while now."

"That's true. I've been teaching for 25 years and you have been a part of my work for over a decade."

"Yes. It's been so great to develop this relationship and see how well the students are doing. Thank you again for agreeing to do this interview with me today. Let's get right to the question if you don't mind. Why did you come to the professional development day over a decade ago?"

"Well, I hated math and hated teaching math. My team encouraged me to go. I said, 'I will try for my students.' I wanted to do this because I needed my students to find joy in math, and quite frankly, I needed to find it as well. I felt it would be different than a new curriculum, and I needed a spark."

"As you learned the instructional strategies what did you discover?"

"I discovered that I actually love teaching math with the instructional strategies that you taught me! The students just make this process so incredible. You might not believe this, but I've asked to teach math every year since that professional development day!"

"That is so cool to hear. What is the most versatile part of it that works in your classroom?

"The strategies create and use a daily stimulus, and that uses a reference task to create rigorous, differentiated math experiences targeting the needs of students in every Quadrant! I mean, I can cover in one lesson, all the differentiated experiences extending to various levels. This increases the confidence and success of the students, and as an added bonus, it decreases student anxiety. Who doesn't want that?"

"Is there anything else that you would like to share?"

"Yes. It leaves some problems and tasks unfinished for long term thinking and learning—and that is the making of a Mathineer! We don't have to rush to find the answer! That way, the pressure of solving everything is off. We need to allow the student to make choices about the math stimulus and tasks they prefer, to engage and motivate. It's life-changing!"

• • •

Rachel

"It is so nice to talk to you. It's been a few months since we chatted. How are you doing?"

"I'm great and really excited to share what has been going on in my classroom with you."

"Yes! I can't wait for you to share with us today. I'll get to it then. What was the toughest part about using these instructional strategies?"

"That's easy. I am a bit of a control freak, and since I am teaching second grade, I need my students to understand the foundations and not stretch past that—even if my students are bored or could handle more. I knew that *I couldn't stretch* my students, not because they lacked the skill or ability, but *that I did*. I was too scared. It was all me."

"Wow! Thank you for being that vulnerable and stating it so boldly. Now that you have been exposed to the strategies, which one do you feel the most comfortable in using, and how does it help?"

"I use open-ended tasks because they extend the content beyond the grade-two standard. Through the open-ended tasks I sometimes gain more depth within grade two, and at other times I can now help my students stretch beyond grade two. I do this with conceptual exploration only."

"This is fantastic. Thank you so much for being willing to share your vulnerability and help out so many more teachers."

"It's my pleasure!"

• • •

Linda

"Linda, you are one busy woman! Thank you so much for taking the time to meet with me today."

"When you called, I was thrilled!"

"That's awesome. Do you remember what I told you after our first observation together? How did that make you feel?"

"Oh, I remember, and I was truly a bit freaked out. I am a linear thinker, so mathematics fits this way of thinking perfectly—or so I thought! Until you showed me some interesting things. I love the linear way that much in math can be done. But when you showed me that it was hindering student thinking, reasoning, sense-making, and extending, I knew that I was the biggest problem in my students' classroom. I was preventing cognitive thinking because I felt the next step had to be done in the only order I had ever been taught."

"I know how hard it was for you to let the linear go and trust in cognitive thinking. But Number Sense is foundational truth. It's all about counting, and so if the numbers are in relational understanding of each other, that is the foundation we can pull from to think around and explore. So, with your willingness to trust the process, where did that take you?"

"Well I started with reference tasks as the base of many of my lessons. Once I started connecting to reference tasks each month, I was able to see the students grasp bigger concepts. The daily stimulus which extends math for all students was a huge key for me. It allowed students to have the power and autonomy to take math to a higher level."

"What is a benefit to this type of thinking and teaching?"

"My students create math questions regularly now. I see how questions push the students to think at the next level. Now my students are challenging my own thinking with their questions and prompts! This is a whole new world."

● ● ●

Karen

"Karen, I want to say right off the bat that the first time I entered into your classroom one word came to mind! BRILLIANT! You knew how to facilitate such a diverse group of students, many of whom had some intense learning challenges."

"Thank you so much for that. I was honored you felt that way. I think I can feel myself blushing. Ha! Thank you again so much."

"You are welcome! So let's cut to the chase with this. Do you remember how you felt when we talked about how you were setting math limits on your students? What happened?"

"I remember thinking, 'I have such a range of student learning, that if I extend too far in the above grade level extremes, I might lose them.'

"What was one thing you implemented, and what happened at that point?"

"I took hold of my fear and used stimuli and tasks to my advantage by asking open-ended questions and offering choices."

"What happened when you offered choices?"

"Offering choices was the key! I was giving a range to the students so we could see where our learning was going. This was exposing the students to higher level math. This was the math that I initially thought was beyond them. But the students totally surprised me! They offered wonderful thinking, and grasp of the content in ways I didn't even know were possible with this diverse group of students."

"Is this something you will carry forward with?"

"Absolutely! This is evidence that motivates me to give more and more, well beyond kindergarten thinking, to my students. They have shown me that they are Mathineers!"

● ● ●

Donald

"Donald, I want to thank you for taking the time today to share your experiences with the different strategies."

"You're welcome."

"When I first saw you work with your students, I noticed that you have a great pedagogy."

"Thank you."

"You're welcome. Can I ask you what you felt was your biggest challenge in working with your students and using the strategies?"

"Sure. After going to the professional development and seeing how to implement things, I noticed right away I had two challenges with my style of teaching. I leave things a little too open ended and too loose. I know I can add a bit more rigor and complexity to things as well, so when we start on a concept, we don't become too stagnant and mundane."

"With that *new awakening* as you call it, what have you changed or added, and what results are you are seeing?"

"I love it when students are working hard on a conceptual piece and they start to push the extensions—all students get super involved. When we don't always worry about the school math side of things, we see great math reasoning and sense-making. The students are creating questions and they are pushing themselves further than I thought was possible."

"With these results what do you hope to accomplish next?"

"I would like to see a few more of my fellow teachers implement them so that we can help more students have success."

"Awesome. Let's involve more teachers and see what can happen."

Teachers! Isn't this incredible? How many of you want to experience the same types of shifts and changes in your classroom? It is totally possible to help students in a way that is ground-level, foundational, cognitive thinking and procedural action. It only takes a few tweaks to make the impact real and create true change. Altogether we saw huge improvements with the teachers, and their goals to create math experiences that touch on the conceptual as well as the procedural activities, thus increasing their Math Ability as well as their Number Sense. This translates to helping the students improve their Math Ability and Number Sense, too. Teachers, are you ready to find success?

15
DALLAS—THE DISCOVERY

"I cannot teach anyone anything. I can only make them think."
—Socrates

DEPLETED. DEFEATED. DISHEARTENED. Disgusted. Depressed. Dying inside from sheer frustration. The alliteration with the letter "d" was somehow satisfying and made me feel more validated as the evidence mounted, the emotions being prompted by my gloomy thoughts as I drove home from another day of teaching, hot tears running down my face. The sky outside was darkening. It would soon rain. I thought, *Why don't kids care? Why don't they get it?*

More tears fell as the miles passed underneath me on my slow drive home. I thought, "All the lesson planning and designing, the months and months of going in early and staying late. I wondered at that moment, *If I couldn't manage all I was doing now, how would I ever be able to have kids and this teaching job*? And what was all of this extra work for? No gains and no results. This was thoroughly frustrating!"

I came to an intersection and listened to the rhythmic pattern of the windshield wipers slap off the late fall rain. All I could see was a speckle of red from the stoplight through the windshield and my mind continued in gloomy reflection. Then I asked the question, "Can I truly keep up this pace? Can I sustain the amount of work? I can't even answer the gifted kids' questions, and I'm not helping the struggling kids either. I'm actually questioning my math skills! I thought I was good at math, but I can't inspire anyone else to get it! The light turned green and I stepped on the gas as I shouted out, "What am I doing? This isn't for me!"

I thought again, *Teaching isn't for me. There is no way I can do this.* My mind raced to my student, Dallas. He was one of the most gifted kids I had ever taught. In my mind's eye I could see his blond hair and thin fingers as he grasped the pencil and drew the models of how he understood math in his mind. He could construct and reason through math concepts academically, and still apply it in a hands-on way, like the time he and his dad built a miniature golf course in his backyard.

He could do things whether I taught him or not. The assessments revealed that. I could give him anything and he would be able to produce an answer. How? His Number Sense was beautiful, and it freaked me out! It was through "teaching" Dallas that I figured out how weak my Number Sense was. It was poorly developed. With each math unit we covered, I was exposed at deeper and deeper levels in not understanding math innately the way Dallas did.

That was the naked truth. That was what I was crying about. I was frustrated because I was vulnerable! I did not know math as well as I thought. Suddenly a memory was forced to the surface as I continued to drive through the rain.

I was back in college, sitting across a large oak desk where a neatly finished stack of corrected papers showed a tinge of red coming from them. My professor's reflection could be seen off the polished surface. A conversational exchange was happening between the two reflected faces. Mine was pulled down and distraught over learning my grade in the class. My professors was a mix of compassion but with the seriousness of having to tell me the truth. "This isn't for you." I was talking with him and trying to figure out my next step. "Miss Zupancic, I see your efforts. I see your determination, and I value the time and work that you put into the subject. But this just isn't working out. I'm sorry," he said, as he handed me my final exam.

My eyes scanned the testing packet over and over. It was as if the paper was taunting me, poking fun at me, mocking me. For over 15 years of my life, I thought I could do math. I knew my facts; I could produce the work. I totally understood it. But, this class! This final math class that was going to lead me to my dream job chopped away at me and left me a splintered, shattered mess. As I continued to look over the test, it confirmed to me that I really didn't understand this type of math. I was at a crossroads.

Besides feeling so humiliated by failing, I was stripped down to my bones because everything I thought about math, especially that I thought I was good at it, was ripped away. I felt exposed. My plan of being an actuary (someone who crunches numbers for insurance companies) was gone. My professor was simply confirming it and trying to give me options. I had to face the truth that I struggled in math.

My head was racked with thoughts. *You are a mimicker. You follow any kind of formula and algorithm. You give the precious answer but actually struggle to explain the why and how of the reasoning behind it!* To quiet the voice in my head I looked back at my professor and slowly stood up. I took in a deep, choking breath and walked out, watching my reflection in the gleam of the oak desk disappear.

The slapping of the rain off the windshield seemed to bring me back to the present, a lifetime away from that college memory. Because of that failed class I had to find something to do with my math major, so I went into teaching. But teaching had merely served to reveal my awful weakness! I simply couldn't do math, let alone teach it. My tight grip on the steering wheel seemed to loosen and let go—like everything else. I found myself in a terrifying place. I'm a math teacher! I can mimic. I know the facts, and I can do any kind of procedure, and yet, I didn't know the *why* of the answers. My student, Dallas, did! He could flip, rotate, or spin the numbers and explain why he did it, and he could apply the appropriate procedures to show the truth of what the numbers meant. Most of all he could represent numbers and expressions in a variety of ways, creating visual models to articulate concepts. It blew me away.

My car seemed to be on autopilot, even in the steady rain, while my head swirled about in this horrible place of vulnerability. My mind kept reflecting on what happened with Dallas. I was teaching about division and fractions, the whole *flip and multiply* procedure. I gave him the problem 8 divided by ½. Dallas looked at the question and reasoned that, logically, if he was to physically take water that was in an 8-gallon jug and pour it into smaller containers, he was going to need more containers.

He was right. I wanted to know why. He explained that if you had ½ gallon containers and needed to physically pour the water in them you would need more than 8 containers. In fact, you would need 16 half-gallon containers. I asked him to show me his thinking. He modeled it right there in the class.

This came naturally to him. He really understood the value of numbers and their relationships. He could not only communicate it, but he could visualize it, model it, and represent it. Many students who are bright (Quadrant II students) can't do this. Most students who *don't* have a strong Number Sense absolutely struggle with this. They will look at that problem and think 8 divided by ½ is 4. They are displaying poor Number Sense and going on the fact that 4 multiplied by 2 is 8; therefore 8 divided by 2 (because they ignore the ½) must be 4. I was stripped down and yet fascinated with how he could know this!

$8 \div \frac{1}{2} = 16$	Students will look at this problem and think 8 divided by ½ is 4. They look at the 8 at the 2 but ignore the fraction. They think the problem is $8 \div 2 = 4$

Three more blocks passed, and I came to a stop sign. I was taken from the memory of my classroom back to my driving. I looked to my left and saw a playground. It was all but empty because of the rain. The wet jungle gym and slides looked sad, lonely, and hopeless, just like I felt.

Then suddenly I saw a mom and her little one in the corner of the playground with an umbrella, raincoats, and Wellingtons. She was smiling . . . no wait . . . she was laughing, and so was the child. I saw that cute kid pump his little legs and leap up in the air and come down with all his might into a puddle, forcing the water outward, causing a huge splash. The puddle game! His arm was fist-pumping in the air to do it again and again.

Just then the car behind me honked, reminding me where my gas pedal was, and it was like a shockwave went through me. As I pushed the gas and moved forward, so did my thoughts. In the bleakness of a cold fall rain, the image of joy and hope started to rise upward from my gut to my chest. *I'm not a quitter! I'm not ready to give up! I'm too invested. There has to be a way. I'll find it,* I thought. Suddenly I started to list things in my head: 1) What do I know? 2) What can I control? 3) What can I not control?

What do I know? I know that I can improve my instructional practices. What can I control? Only what happens in my classroom. What can I not control? Everything outside of my classroom—parents, home life, whether or not homework gets done,—blaming circumstances for student outcomes. I could feel the pull of negative thoughts wanting me to get sucked back into frustration. *No! Wait! Let's go back to what can I do to improve my classroom. Stay here,* I kept coaching myself, *stay in the possibility. Ok, ok. What can I do? I can improve my instructional practices. Yes! Ok, that's right, but how?* One more city block splashed by underneath my car.

I thought, *I need to find real professional development. I need to find ways to help kids understand what I'm teaching—no wait, not only to understand but to experience it. Just like that little one I saw with the puddle. He will remember that day for the rest of his life! Because he was able to experience it. Yes. Right.* Now for the crazy thinking. *I want to do it in less time and with more joy. I'm done with all this planning that ends up being a waste of time and getting me nowhere. I want student engagement. I want student outcomes. I want them to experience math!*

Suddenly I had a purpose again. I was on a mission to find great training and to develop something radical so that kids could *experience* math, exactly like that little kid was experiencing the puddle—in very hands (Wellingtons)-on, physical, mental, and emotional way. I was going to create this for my students. I was going to find the best practices, learn how the brain learns, and learn task-rich experiences so my students could really "get it!"

As I rounded the last bend and turned left into my subdivision, I drove with direction and purpose. I was centered. I was focused. My depleted energy was restored. My defeated heart was filled with possibilities. My disheartened attitude was suddenly filled with confidence. I was no longer disgusted with myself, and I felt encouraged. Depression and frustration were replaced with hope and a sense of real action.

I pulled into my driveway. There were no more tears. My face was no longer red and blotchy. I was smiling, feeling that I had the power to truly change everything. I put the van into park, turned off the key, and grabbed my notebook. In the driveway, I started to capture all the ideas and thoughts I had had during the last half of the drive. *There I thought, look what you can do Rebekkah! You, Rebekkah, can do anything you set your mind to!*

16
GOING BEYOND PLAYING SCHOOL

WAIT A MINUTE—REBEKKAH? Do you mean Chapter 4, Rebekkah? Yes. Spoiler alert! I am Rebekkah.

Why Rebekkah? Well, as a little girl I hated my name, Jonily. Jonily meant a spotlight shining right on me, and I didn't want to be noticed. I didn't want to have any kind of attention the name generated. I hated how people would struggle with the pronunciation, the spelling of my name, and honestly, I didn't have time for it! I always thought Rebekkah was a much better choice. So, as you read in Chapter 4 and 15, Rebekkah was really me.

But now, I love my name, Jonily Zupancic. (And if you want to know how to say my last name, it's zoo-pan-sick). It's a great conversation starter, people remember it, and I love having this unique identity.

The facts in Chapter 4 are true. I was an apartment kid. I had moved to five different apartments by the time I was in the fifth grade. I smelled like smoke, I wore glasses, and I was a little frumpy. I was a tiny gymnast, short, petite, and nimble. I was quiet, but not shy. I could speak my mind. I knew I was going somewhere. I could just feel it. A side note: I love rules unless they are stupid.

Back to the point. Through teaching, I discovered the depth of my math flaws. It was hard to be so vulnerable—the math teacher who doesn't know math. I will also confess to you that I did not want to write this book and reveal all that I wasn't to the world, but I knew that going through the journey would help thousands more than I could ever reach in the classroom or through my workshops. I wanted to reach every teacher everywhere and show them the story of how I became a Mathineer!

As luck would have it, as I was finishing writing this book, I was able to connect with a fellow teacher. We hadn't been in contact for a few months, and we usually only talk once or twice a year at my spring masterclass. I received a phone call from her, in which she shared all about where she is in her mathematical journey with teaching students. She focuses on special education students. Through the conversation she asked me what I was up to. I told with her I was writing this book, *Making Mathineers.* She was very intrigued, so I took her on a fast journey through what I had been experiencing.

I shared with her the concept of the Quadrants and the story of one of the students who is featured in this book, whom she already knew, Brian. She was surprised that he was going to be a feature in the book. We both had known his emotional and behavioral challenges, and that he hadn't passed a state math test in years—that is until he started working with me and the instructional practices taught in this book, which I use to help students increase their Number Sense and Math Ability.

She was interested and wanted more, so I continued. I shared that the bulk of the focus with Brian had been to help him with his social and behavioral needs, not math intervention. As I worked with him through the use of target questions and the achievement strategies, I was able to uncover that he had a strong conceptual understanding of mathematics but was weak in his procedural understanding of math. This is why he landed in Quadrant IV.

The reason he has never passed a math test given by the teacher or state was that he couldn't *articulate the conceptual math in a procedural way,* the school math way. For Brian, his ability to do mental math and how he understood relationships with numbers were solid! However, he did not have the ability to understand the language of math he needed to break down his Number Sense into procedures that were accepted in school.

Brian needed language to express how he thought, and also *math language* to be able to express his understanding procedurally. But that was not happening, and none of his answers would match what he actually knew. The result was that Brian was not only carrying around labels like *emotionally challenged,* and *behaviorally challenged*, he was dubbed a third label of *weak in math.*

As I continued to relate this story, my fellow teacher became intrigued by what she was hearing and wanted to know the *solution* for Brian. He needed language to help him successfully connect what he knew conceptually, and to be able to express it procedurally.

I went on to explain to my fellow teacher that Brian needed to be taught procedures, but not *out of context or unconnected from his conceptual understanding.* That was the key! The context and connection of what he knew conceptually must be first be in order to develop the procedure to express it.

Teachers must realize that when they have uncovered the student's understanding, they must use the student's language to connect the concepts to the notation of the procedures. Having the connection that we use in traditional mathematics allows a student to more easily move into Quadrant I. However, there needs to be consistency in this delivery. Teachers can't uncover the conceptual and then teach a procedure, thinking that it solved the student's math challenges. No, this must be done with *each new concept*, using the strategies I taught in chapter 11, to build procedural ability.

Teachers who tap into a student's conceptual understanding and connect it to what it looks like symbolically and procedurally in mathematics, are in essence, *Making Mathineers*. No matter if students begin in Quadrant II, III, or IV, we have learned that through:

- target questions to assess and place in a Quadrant,
- providing a stimulus to promote reasoning and sense making,
- removing the noise to allow for student autonomy and choice in solving,

students will be able to share their thinking.

Some of our favorite ways to get students to share are with these prompts:

- "What do you see?
- "What do you notice?
- "Tell me about..."

As teachers see this type of interaction and exchange, in all the excitement we need to hold back giving the answers and merely keep asking first. One last emphasis, teachers. Don't jump in too quickly. Allow students to struggle and watch the magic of making a *Mathineer*. If students aren't allowed to wrestle with problems, they won't be so proud of finding solutions.

The conversation continued, "This type of instruction is powerful because, as each new concept is taught with the achievement formula, both conceptual and procedural learning will stay with the student." She asked, "Does this work with Quadrant III students?" "Yes!" I said with a ton of excitement in my voice. I shared with her a few stories of the Quadrant III students I had worked with, and what their improvements had shown.

My fellow teacher was blown away by what I was divulging. I could tell in the tone of her voice that she wanted to fire off many more questions to know *how* and *what* I was doing to get these outcomes. But instead, she asked, "How do we get parents and other teachers to get out of the procedural versus conceptual war they are in?" I was ready for this answer and responded, "If we only focus students on procedures, eventually they will hit concepts that stop them in their tracks, and they will have no foundation to stand on—there will be a mathematical breakdown."

She jumped right in at this opportunity and said, "That is so true! This completely happened to me. I was good at math up until I started algebra. Up to that point I knew all the answers; I could do any math they asked me to do, but with algebra, I quickly discovered I didn't *know* anything." This was a familiar story I had heard over and over again.

She expressed this that started her on her search for what we call Number Sense. I did not respond, but let her continue. She became super excited, and expressed that she was a Quadrant II, "false positive" student. Once again, she had opened the door to having a deep and beautiful conversation, so I took the opportunity and confessed something as well.

"Did you know that I had a similar mathematical breakdown?" She was taken aback. "Really?" came her reply.

"Oh yes." I shot back. "Mine happened in college. Up to that point, I had one more major course to pass for my specific degree. But I failed. Not by a little smidgeon, but by a landslide. It was an epic fail."

She was stunned. I shared with her that because of my failure, I stopped the pursuit of my passion—my dream job. And I went into teaching. "But," I told her, "the breakdown of what I thought I knew about math was really stripped away to the foundation while I was in my third year of teaching. That was the year I taught a student named Dallas."

I explained that he was a Quadrant I student. Dallas basically shattered my mathematical foundation, but instead of only crying about it, I decided to harvest how he thought about math. I needed to be taught so that I could actually make a difference in the students I was teaching.

Dallas came into my class and I was blown away by what he knew conceptually, and how he could also explain and apply it procedurally. I would ask him to "show me his thinking" again and again. Through this process, I developed *target questions,* then different strategies. Soon I began to notice other Quadrant I students. I saw how they learned, and I developed more and more strategies from what they taught me. Eventually all of this led to the creation of the Achievement Formula that I use to help thousands of students. (Look for this book in the near future).

As we were ending the conversation, we both discussed the importance of helping the Quadrant II students—those *false-positive* kiddos that are master mimickers and fast with their facts, so they won't slip through each grade, learning less and less, until they hit their mathematical breakdown. When that breakdown hits, they start to think they are dumb. Like me, they'll wonder, *what happened, I thought I was good at math, but I stink at it.*

She agreed, was inspired to read *Making Mathineers,* and decided to attend the spring masterclass. I expressed how great it was to talk to her, and for all she is doing with her students. I thanked her for sharing her mathematical breakdown story with me as well. Her willingness to be vulnerable meant a great deal to me, about trusting our friendship. It was a powerful conversation and I'll treasure it forever.

Just like the conversation I had with my friend, the discovery of false-positive students happens with others in conferences and professional development workshops that I host. I find that Quadrant II students many times are the bulk of the students in school. They know how to *play school* because they can mimic procedures and they know a lot of math facts, but when they are tasked to express and explain the math, they feel threatened and scared. Many math teachers were Quadrant II kids as well, which makes it difficult to deliver math instruction in any other way than how they had been taught.

Think about the current math war happening in schools and districts. I'm sure you have heard of terms like *old math versus new math,* or *procedural versus conceptual.* Many times, it is the parents of children in school that will post something online about the math homework they are trying to help their child with. The question they are asking may be about the math concept and not just "What's the answer?" The parent is trying to help the student explain his or her thinking, and that is when something is triggered deep in the parent, a realization that there are many different ways to get to a mathematical answer. That is threatening, and when someone feels threatened, they sometimes become defensive and lash out.

Suddenly teachers are being attacked for their math instruction and the reasons they are making children perform math in a certain way. Parents will argue, "Why can't you do math the regular way." As I have taught over the past 20 years in hundreds of different schools, I know that procedural math, or school math, is more likely to be praised than conceptual. But again, the argument is not old math versus new math or procedural versus conceptual. The answer is that we need students to know both! And like we have shown throughout this book they learn how to do this through mathematical experiences.

In chapter 15, the story of me driving home feeling defeated is true. The story of failing my college class—also absolutely true. It was the beginning of my mathematical journey that turned into a true achievement and became the Achievement Formula. Let me just reiterate that pushing through the fear to find the answers was not fun, but the result has been something I never knew could be achieved!

Wins for Students:

- At the end of grade 6, in less than one year of learning this instructional model with his teacher, having used the Achievement Formula, the key to Making Mathineers, Brian passed the state assessment in math for the first time in his life!

- Mary "broke the bell curve" on the standardized assessment. Wha??? She, as well as every second grader in this group of students, scored in the 70th percentile or higher (50th percentile is average).

- Holly saw her Number Sense begin to increase and she was having less and less confusion procedurally.

- Adam learned how to chunk sets of a pattern so that he could count efficiently the number of blocks in each chunk and then add those numbers together. Brilliant!

Wins for Teachers:

- Linda stopped forcing all of the linear and step-by-step processes of math, and now allows the experiences to build, increasing her mathematical knowledge.

- Liz left her fear behind and went all in, teaching by the Achievement Formula, and adding more and more math experiences to help her students quickly grow.

- Karen learned that offering choices was the key! Choices gave a range to the students so she could see where their learning was taking them. She said, "This was math I initially thought was beyond them. But the students totally surprised me! They offered wonderful thinking and grasped the content in ways I didn't even know were possible with such a diverse group of students.

- Jennifer stopped marking her retirement calendar, and she looked forward to engaging with her students. She said that she didn't want it to end because she knew she was finally making a difference.

Teachers, what will be your win? After going through all the stories of the students, the testimonies of the teachers, learning how to use target questions, discovering how to get rid of noise, and removing the questions, to exposing the students to math experiences through using the 120 chart, folding paper, making rectangles, discovering that subtraction is distance and division is counting, has math changed for you? What will be your takeaway, and are you hungering for more?

Remember this question: What is a Mathineer? A Mathineer is a person who thinks through math. They find relationships with numbers by tapping into their existing Number Sense.

Teachers, you are key in making the Mathineer by delivering instruction, providing math experiences, prompting questions, and promoting thinking and reasoning.

You have the exponential effect of helping students move to Quadrant I and enhancing their position as a Mathineer. You have been exposed to many of the tools to do this, because within each student is a Mathineer. The final question is, are you brave enough to let go of your math fear and help them become true Mathineers?

MAKING MATHINEERS

What is the secret for helping students increase their Number Sense and Math Ability?

Minds on Math presents a transformational online course, targeting lesson design and delivery to improve student engagement, understanding, and retention of content. It is called:

Making Mathineers

This online course is designed for pre-k through grade 12 math teachers, intervention specialists, instructional coaches, principals, curriculum leaders and instructional leaders in schools which are struggling to meet the math needs of the diverse variety of math students.

Making Mathineers uses the right *instructional delivery system* to help you make a lasting impact.

*Making Mathineer*s is designed for *all students* to gain access to the same high levels of mathematics because the focus is on *where* the student is, then engaging them in such a way to *extract their thinking* and then *move* them closer to becoming Mathineers!

Students and teachers will gain math confidence by using Making Mathineers. How? By implementing the *instructional strategies* that have the power to increase conceptual math learning as well as procedural learning. This is the impact that will increase the student's Number Sense and Math Ability.

Benefits:
- Learn how to teach more in less time with fewer planning hours and minimal stress.
- Plan ONE lesson that meets the needs of ALL students at ANY ability level.
- Identify current level of student math understanding and misunderstanding with quick, targeted math questions and prompts.
- Impact student success, confidence, and achievement with ease by implementing five simple strategies and increasing the complexity of each strategy over time.

This course is an enhancement to every math curriculum resource, and it is the game-changer you have been waiting for. Visit the website today and get started on the journey of creating math experiences that will transform student thinking, reasoning and long-term understanding. www.makingMathineers.com

Jonily Zupancic, is an expert in mathematics instruction, assessment and intervention. She is a speaker, coach and consultant who helps schools and inspires teachers to enhance math instruction at the elementary, middle and high school levels targeting the diverse needs of all students so that teachers and students can become Mathineers! Improvement systems focus on providing rich math experiences, high level delivery methods and differentiated classroom structures. Jonily lives in Ohio with her husband, Ryan, and two sons.

YOU HAVE TO

CHANGE

BEHAVIOR

BEFORE

BELIEF

-JONILY ZUPANCIC
WWW.MINDSONMATH.COM

"IF I SAY IT
THEY HEAR IT.
IF THEY SAY IT,
THEY LEARN IT."

Jonily Zupancic
www.jonily.com

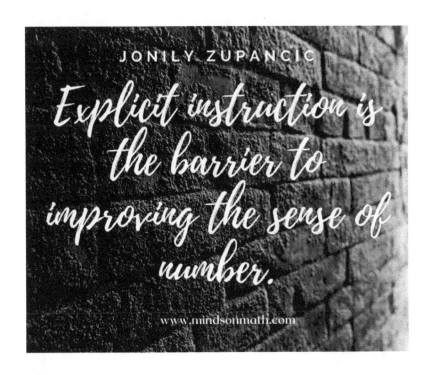

JONILY ZUPANCIC

Explicit instruction is the barrier to improving the sense of number.

www.mindsonmath.com

Number sense can't be taught, but number sense can be learned and improved overtime and through experience.

THE ACHIEVEMENT FORMULA
www.mindsonmath.com/AchievementFormula

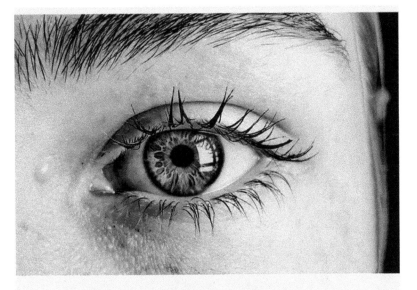

You can't change what you do without changing how you think.

WORKS CITED

Ariel Starr, Melissa E. Libertus, Elizabeth M. Brannon. 2013. "Number sense in infancy predicts mathematical abilities in childhood,." *Proceedings of the National Academy of Sciences,* 10.1073/pnas.1302751110/-/DCSupplemental.

Florian Cajoi, Ifrah, Gerorges. 2019. *Wikipedia.* December 7. Accessed March 23, 2020. https://en.wikipedia.org/wiki/Mathematical_notation.

Halberda, Melissa E. Libertus Lisa Feigenson Justin. 2011. *Preschool acuity of the approximate number system correlates with school math ability.* August 2. Accessed 2 2019, December. https://onlinelibrary.wiley.com/doi/full/10.1111/j.1467-7687.2011.01080.x.

Justin Halberda, Ryan Ly, Jeremy B. Wilmer, Daniel Q. Naiman, and Laura Germine. 2012. "Number sense across the lifespan as revealed by a massive Internet-based sample." *PNAS* 109 (28) 11116-11120.

Lisa DeNike. 2011. "John Hopkins University." *John Hopkins University.* August 8. Accessed December 2, 2019. https://

releases.jhu.edu/2011/08/08/you-can-count-on-this-math-ability-is-inborn-johns-hopkins-psychologist-finds/.

van Garderen, D., & Montague, M. 2003. "Visual-spatial representation, mathematical problem solving, and students of varying abilities." *Learning Disabilities Research & Practice* 18, 246-254.

Zhang, D., Ding, Y., Stegall, J., & Mo, L. 2012. "The effect of visual-chunking-representation accommodation on geometry testing for students with math disabilities." *Learning Disabilities Research & Practice,* 27, 167-177.

CPSIA information can be obtained
at www.ICGtesting.com
Printed in the USA
FSHW021335230121